GENERATE MORE LE/
AND BUILD A S

EXPLOSIVE
SALES GROWTH
IN REAL ESTATE

EXPLOSIVE SALES GROWTH IN REAL ESTATE

Generate More Leads, Take More Listings, and Build a Six-Figure Income

Paperback ISBN: 978-1-7320979-0-2
Kindle ISBN: 978-1-7320979-1-9

Cover Design: Dino Marino
Interior Design: Christina Gorchos, 3CsBooks.com

What the experts are saying:

"I believe in *The Miracle Equation:* Unwavering Faith + Extraordinary Effort = Miracles (aka "Extraordinary Results"). The principles and scripts in this book should provide you with the Unwavering Faith that the techniques work. Now it's up to you to apply the Extraordinary Effort to build the business and life of your dreams, and create the Extraordinary Results that will transform your business, and your life."
— Hal Elrod, #1 Best-Selling Author of *The Miracle Morning*

"Creating wealth starts with creating income. Explosive Sales Growth in Real Estate will show you how to focus your lead generation to create revenue and keep your profits. Then you can invest!"
— David Osborn - New York Times, Wall Street Journal, and USA Today Best-Selling Author of *Wealth Can't Wait*

"Ryan understands the business of real estate at the deepest level. His coaching has made my growth from 8 to 200+ transactions easier in the past two years. Explosive Sales Growth teaches all the techniques, scripts, and tools an agent needs to be successful. Do yourself a favor and buy this book for your whole team or office."
— Lisa Chinatti - Chinatti Realty Group - Over $2 Million in GCI in 2017

"90% of the people you speak with will not be selling their home this year. Learn to take 'No' in stride and create a plan to get past the 'No' to find your 'Yes'. Explosive Sales Growth in Real Estate provides you the mindset and techniques to move past 'No'."
— Andrea Waltz - Best-Selling Author of *Go for No*

"Ryan teaches the principles of mastering mindset and developing a lead generation strategy that will take your real estate business to the next level. All that's left is for you to read and implement."
— Rock Thomas - International Speaker and Best-Selling Author

A SPECIAL INVITATION FROM RYAN

Having mentored thousands of agents as a real estate sales trainer and coach, I understand the importance of accountability and community when implementing any new strategies. As a co-author of *The Miracle Morning for Salespeople*, I have seen the power a supportive online community provides when building new habits.

I am personally inviting you to join our online community of like-minded salespeople to share ideas and learn from one another during the process of implementing the strategies in this book.

Just go to **www.explosivesalesgrowth.com/community** and request to join the Explosive Sales Growth Community online. The people in this community are dedicated to building a real estate business that supports the life of their dreams.

I will be moderating the community and checking in regularly. I look forward to seeing you there!

DEDICATION

This book is dedicated to the real estate agents, coaches, and mentors that helped me to learn and implement these strategies in my own team and in my coaching. I hope this book helps you to continue to grow your real estate business.

A special thanks to all of the amazing people who contributed insights and interviews. With your support this book will impact the business of thousands of agents for years to come.

Table of Contents

Introduction xi

PART I – PREPARATION

Chapter 1
Mindset and Attitude 1

Chapter 2
Daily Success Ritual 7

Chapter 3
Build Your Database 17

Chapter 4
Know Your Market 25

PART II – LEAD GENERATION – BUILDING THE BUSINESS

Chapter 5
It Starts with Your Sphere 35

Chapter 6
Vendor Referral Network 47

Chapter 7
Social Media 53

Chapter 8
Online Leads 63

Chapter 9
Secondary Transactions 73

Chapter 10

Effective Open Houses 85

Chapter 11

Just Listed and Just Sold 95

Chapter 12

Farming 103

Chapter 13

FSBO (For Sale By Owner) 115

Chapter 14

Expired Listings 125

Chapter 15

Working with Investors 133

Chapter 16

Measure Your Return 139

End of Book Notes 145
Special Invitation 147
About the Author 149

DEVELOPING A SIX-FIGURE MINDSET

The number $100,000 is not an arbitrary number. I chose six figures because it appears for many people to be an unattainable milestone. At the least, it's one of many ceilings that people must break through on their way to the top.

Only the top 8 percent of people in the United States will earn over $100K in a year. Over time, that number will increase based on inflation, but when the number becomes irrelevant, the theories on how to break through the ceiling will remain. This book will give you the tools to develop a thriving real estate business, so you can attain your personal and business goals.

While this task of earning $100,000 may be impossible in some careers, it's an extremely viable goal and even a stepping-stone for anyone working in real estate sales. Sales offers a unique opportunity to earn unlimited income, and real estate celebrates especially large commissions, making the feat even more achievable.

That's not to say you will reach this milestone without hard work. You will need to follow a plan and invest your time, effort, and energy. There are no guarantees. As a recruiter and trainer of real estate salespeople, I have seen nearly one-third of all new agents give up in their first year. After all, this is sales. But with that risk comes great reward. I wrote this book for those who are willing to follow the plan and break through their own personal ceilings.

If you haven't reached the $100K mark yet, this chapter will explore how you can get there.

"What if I already broke through the $100K ceiling?"

If you have already broken through the six-figure income barrier, let the title act as a metaphor for breaking through your next ceiling.

Then pick your next big goal and use the strategies in this book to help you get there. Only the top 1 percent earn over $300K per year, so maybe that's your milestone to shoot for. Regardless of your specific goal, every next step starts with generating more business. At some point we will need to add leverage to the conversation, but for now, let's generate enough business to create the capital to hire that leverage.

If you have never seen me run a training or workshop before, then I should clarify something quickly. Though I believe in the importance of mindset and energy, and I teach the importance of getting them both set straight, you will learn that I am a "meat and potatoes" kind of guy. I want to get straight to the how-to's, tips and tricks so you can implement right away.

There are several proven models to generate results in real estate deals. This book will help you develop a plan tailored specifically to you that will help you hit your sales goals.

While there are eleven different lead generation tools explained in the book, you need only implement three of your choosing. And if you work to master even one, you will find extraordinary success.

Throughout the book, you will find additional suggested resources and tools to help you in growing a business that meets and exceeds your goals. These tools are provided to help you master a particular method that works best for you.

DO NOT attempt to master all of the tools. Not only is it unnecessary, but it will hinder your ability to succeed in any one area. We want to focus your attention and efforts and not water down your work by trying to do too many things.

So, if you are looking to take your real estate career and your income to the next level, then let's take a look at how this book will help you lay out the plan and start executing immediately.

PART I: Preparation

Chapter 1: Mindset and Attitude

The way you approach your business will directly impact your results. There are three important mindset pieces to cover here:

You aren't just a real estate agent. You are a real estate salesperson. You can be the greatest agent (a.k.a. fiduciary) in the world, but if you cannot attract clients, then your business and impact will be extremely limited.

You must maintain faith in the plan you choose. Implement and commit to the action plan.

You must clearly understand why you are getting out of bed every day and following your plan, especially on the days you don't feel like it. How will it impact your business? Your life? Your clients? Your family?

Chapter 2: Daily Success Ritual

This may be one of the most important steps in the whole book. This process allows you to create habits. The daily ritual allows you to stop struggling over whether or not you will take action and makes the crucial daily steps part of a routine you won't even have to think about. You must make lead generation and growing your business a part of your daily routine. As the co-author of The Miracle Morning for Salespeople, I am a huge proponent of a morning routine for success. That whole book was about building a morning routine that allows you to grow personally so you can grow your business. The automaticity of routine will unleash strength and power as you work to accomplish goals you did not know you could achieve, one step at a time, every single day.

Chapter 3: Build Your Database

Again, as a real estate agent, you are in sales. The amount of real estate deals you close directly correlates to how many real estate conversations you hold each day. With that in mind, you must build and maintain a database to consistently and efficiently reach your prospective clients in order to grow relationships. The database should create organization, some automation, and accountability to ensure these real estate conversations happen daily. Throughout this book, we will look at ways to grow your business, along with showing you how to offer value in those conversations so people look forward to speaking with you.

Chapter 4: Know Your Market

We must build a value proposition for our clients. Having access to information is no longer enough. Long ago in a galaxy far, far away, we were the gatekeepers of listing information. People had to come to real estate agents to find out what homes were for sale and for how much. Buyers can find much of this information themselves online these days. However, you will still need to not only know the local market but how to communicate what is happening within it and grasp how it will affect your clients and your business. Your pay will be commensurate to the value you provide to your clients.

PART II: Lead Generation—Building the Business

Chapter 5: It Starts with Your Sphere

Some people get nervous when we talk about calling people you already know. The truth is, they are more likely to work with you because they already know, like, and trust you. If you have no one in your life that knows, likes, and trusts you, then real estate is probably not the right career choice.

It's fun to help friends and family members find their dream homes. Some of these people will be your best referral sources. Even the ones who don't buy or sell from you this year will know people who will. We will work on placing your focused attention on developing this inner circle. It will be the most profitable part of your business since the cost per lead is almost zero.

For those of you who are not new to the business and have sold some homes, this is equally, if not more, important for you. Past clients are part of your sphere of influence. In fact, they may be the most important, since they already trusted you enough to work with you. Don't orphan your past clients.

Chapter 6: Vendor Referral Network

One thing we know for sure is that every homeowner will, in the near future, have a project to complete or maintenance required at their home. One way you can provide value for your clients is to connect them with great vendors with a shared commitment to quality work and customer service. Done properly, these vendor programs should create a steady flow of referrals for both you and your vendors. Learn these tips and strategies to create a regular flow of referrals.

Chapter 7: Social Media

With the all-consuming Internet and the wake of social media apps—including Facebook, Twitter, Instagram, LinkedIn, and Google +, not to mention the ones we haven't even seen yet—it's hard to deny that social media will play a powerful role in business and consumer decisions for a long time.

Social media networks are powerful tools, but most salespeople use them incorrectly. There is a hint to a successful social media strategy in the name: "social." We must develop a consistent program of interacting with people on social media. Learn how to develop social content that people want to interact with to generate more business.

Social media is powerful in many ways, and we will discuss strategies for three of them in this chapter. You will increase brand recognition by consistently staying in front of your target audience. You will capture leads by creating content that people will value enough to provide you with their contact information. You will listen for opportunity. People will say things on social media to complete strangers that you as a real estate agent would pay to know, like when they get engaged, get married, get pregnant, have a new child, etc. Life-altering events often prompt home buying decisions.

Chapter 8: Online Leads

There are several ways to generate leads online. Since over 90 percent of buyers start their property search online, it is no surprise that online leads have grown to become one of the top sources of business for real estate agents. Each of the different types of online leads have their own special nuances, so we will discuss the various options, including your own website leads through search engine optimization (SEO), content strategy and pay-per-click (PPC) traffic, along with paid online leads through third-party sites used in the home search. We will also discuss how to use email marketing with these leads.

Chapter 9: Secondary Transactions

I consider secondary transactions to be any transaction created because of another transaction. There are many opportunities agents often fail to recognize for generating new sales from business they already have. Learn how to generate more business from your current listings and buyer clients.

Chapter 10: Effective Open Houses

Open houses are one of several ways to create secondary transactions. However, open houses do not just have to be from your own listings. New agents can build an entire business with the right open house strategies for covering open houses for other agents. This chapter will teach you the tips and scripts to generate and convert open house leads into buyer and seller clients.

Chapter 11: Just Listed and Just Sold

While this is another way to generate more business through marketing your seller listings, there is a lot more to working just listed and just sold homes. You may contact people about a newly-sold property on their street as a comparative sale for what their home may be worth. You don't even have to be the agent who sold the home. There are opportunities to mix prospecting and marketing here to drive your business. In this chapter, you will learn the scripts and marketing tools to maximize just listed and just sold properties.

Chapter 12: Farming

Farming has long been a tactic in real estate lead generation. Take advantage of the economies of scope by targeting the same group of individuals through multiple marketing and prospecting tools. Soon, your mailers, open houses, and signs will all be in the same neighborhood. Your presence in the local market will help strengthen your brand and establish you as the market expert.

While you typically may farm with direct mail campaigns to a certain neighborhood or demographic, there are ways to include your farms in various other lead generation activities. You can incorporate tips from the chapters on just listed and just sold properties, open houses, and social media. On top of mailing once a month to your farm, imagine Facebook posts and ads that target just your preferred neighborhoods. Then, what if you called homeowners to let them know each time a new home hit the market or sold in their neighborhood? These are opportunities to turn the people in your farm into members of your sphere of influence by building the relationship.

Chapter 13: FSBO (For Sale By Owner)

If you do not have a strong sphere of influence in your area of business, then learning to find immediate business is a must. While converting FSBO to clients may not be easy, they are often easy to find, and they all have one thing in common: they want to sell their house. In fact, they have typically taken out ads or at least posted a sign to let you know, "I want to sell my house."

What they are also letting you know is that they don't believe you offer enough value to pay you a commission, which is why they are listing it themselves. This is an objection we will need to learn to overcome, but the truth is that very few FSBOs make it to the closing table without an agent. In this chapter, we will discuss how to present your value without asking for the listing so when they are ready to list, the client will choose to list with you.

Chapter 14: Expired Listings

Expired listing leads have one thing in common with FSBO leads: they both have raised their hand as someone who wants to sell their house. The approach to landing them as clients may be slightly different, though, since the expired listing leads have hired an agent in the past.

Think about that. They hired an agent to sell their home, and their home didn't sell. My guess is the agent told them they could sell this home for such-and-such agreed-upon price. In many cases, they likely over-promised and under-delivered. It doesn't mean the agent was a bad agent. It could be the seller was unrealistic about price and the agent accepted instead of declining the listing. Maybe there were repairs that were unknown until after an inspection. Whatever the reason, what matters more than the reason is how the seller feels about why the home didn't sell.

This chapter will teach you how to listen to expired leads, overcome their objections and concerns, and land the listing. Beyond merely taking the listing, though, you will also be helping them understand your goal of meeting or exceeding their expectations. You will need to show them the proof to get them on course.

Chapter 15: Working with Investors

Investors make great clients because they will become super-charged repeat clients in an industry where referrals are far more lucrative than repeat business. Imagine a restaurant where the manager comes out to the table at the end of the meal and says:

"We're so happy you came to try out our new place. What did you think?"

The customer responds with a smile, "We loved it. The food was some of the best we have had. The service was impeccable, and the views are amazing. We can't wait to come back."

"We look forward to seeing you again soon," the manager responds with pride.

"You can count on it. We should be back in seven to ten years."

That is the real estate industry in a nutshell. When it comes to owner-occupied homes, you can expect that repeat clients will occur only after many years in most cases. Referrals from these clients can drive your business, but that is a different chapter.

Investors, on the other hand, tend to buy multiple properties. The average flipper buys and sells four or more homes in a year. Buy-and-hold investors often buy more units each year or sell their current smaller units to build up to larger, more profitable complexes. This means more commissions to help grow your business. This chapter will teach the strategies of how to find and serve these clients to grow your real estate business.

Chapter 16: Measure Your Return

There are countless agents who have built a large real estate business based on volume, but they have little to nothing to show for all their hard work at the end of the year. Investing in your own real estate business offers one of the greatest opportunities for return on investment if, and only if, you hold the money you invest in your lead generation accountable. Many agents fail to measure and track their marketing and prospecting dollars in a way that allows them to make sound business decisions. In order to scale and grow a business that will provide the lifestyle you are looking for, it is imperative that we measure our results, determine our return on investment, and make spending decisions based on this information. This chapter will highlight the tools and techniques for measuring your results and making sound spending decisions.

Chapter 1

MINDSET AND ATTITUDE

A s humans, we all have the desire to meet one of two objectives at all times: seek pleasure and avoid pain. Seems simple enough, right? In fact, those two simple objectives have likely kept us around for thousands of years. Avoiding pain starts as soon as we learn to stop doing things like putting our hand on a hot stovetop. Seeking pleasure drives sex appeal, reproduction, and all human existence.

You are probably wondering what the hell this has to do with real estate. Let me explain. Sales , in general, is not for the faint of heart. We should prepare for the ups and downs. We should expect to hear "no" from people. We should understand that not every call, door-knock, mailer, or Facebook ad turns immediately into business. We should know some deals fall apart and never make it to the closing table.

Some of you are still wondering what sales and real estate have to do with one another. You're saying, "I'm a real estate agent." Or, "I am a fiduciary." And I want to share with you that this is only a small percentage of your job. In most cases, what you have learned on your licensing exam will only cover the fiduciary duties. Typical new agents are never taught how to find business. This one little shift in mindset will determine your effectiveness at building a successful real estate business.

Successful Agents are Salespeople

Your real estate business requires a steady stream of new clients. That, my friend, makes you a salesperson. Anybody who wants to build a business at a high level needs to not only be great at their job, but they need to become a master at finding leads and converting those leads into clients. As soon as you absolutely understand the importance of that statement and allow it to affect your daily activities, you will see a tremendous impact on the growth of your business.

At some point, if you follow the lead generation strategies in this book, you will grow your business to a place where you need to add leverage. You will likely build a team around you to complete multiple tasks of keeping your clients well taken care of so you can focus all of your attention on the most important task of continuing to fill your pipeline with business.

I always let my coaching clients know if they intend to grow a team and build a business rather than a job, then they had better learn to love their lead generation. You will likely be the most effective lead generation member on your team. You will need to lead by example, and the more time you free up from other tasks, the more time you will spend on finding new clients.

None of this should discourage you. In fact, having clarity around the most important part of your job should make it easier for you to succeed. There is no question that lead generation is the most important part of your job.

We Are Not All Ants Marching

You may notice that there are eleven different lead generation tactics explained in this book. There are even more options out there, but these tried-and-true methods will grow your real estate business. You must not attempt to master all eleven methods. I repeat: do not try all methods of lead generation.

Here's the deal: if you attempt all of these methods of lead generation, you will no doubt spread yourself too thin. At best, you will implement them all in a mediocre fashion, if you have any time left to implement anything after all of your time spent learning. No doubt you may need to test a few to find the ones that resonate with you, but you should focus on mastering only two or three of the strategies. If you look across almost any industry, specialists earn far more than generalists. Similarly, you are not looking to become the jack of all trades and master of none.

The goal is to find lead generation strategies that fit your personality, your strengths, and your goals. Then we will build a learning plan and an action plan based on those techniques. The great news is that these techniques have worked for agents in the past. Agents I coach or have coached in the past use these techniques successfully. They are all proven methods with proven results. Several of these clients are earning multiple six-figure incomes and some even seven-figure incomes. Mastering any one of these should allow you to hit or surpass your six-figure income goal, but we want to master two or three methods so we don't have all our eggs in one basket.

You Must Have Faith in the System

In my last book, *The Miracle Morning for Salespeople*, Hal Elrod and I talked about Hal's miracle equation. The equation states simply: Miracles = Unwavering Faith + Extraordinary Effort

None of these lead generation techniques will work without both elements. Several of the techniques take time, and some take an investment of cash. You must have faith, stay committed to the process, and put the effort into completing the activities to create success. While I know these methods will all allow you to build a six-figure business, the systems don't work if you don't put in the effort.

I hope you will read each chapter of this book. You will learn the basics about several lead generation techniques. You will determine the methods that best fit your goals and strengths. Then you will dive into only a couple and master them. We have even provided you with additional resources and tools for each of the techniques, including scripts and dialogues, technology, additional videos and information, and coaching programs that will help you achieve mastery.

> **Access these resources at**
> **www.ExplosiveSalesGrowth.com/RealEstate.**

The questions you should consider are these:

Knowing these lead generation methods work and have worked for many other agents before you, how long are you willing to commit to the process to achieve your goals?

Do you have 100 percent faith in yourself to implement these activities? Are you willing to accept the pain of stepping out of your comfort zone in lead generation to seek the pleasure of achieving your business and income goals?

Do You Still Want to Do This? Why?

I promise that there will be days when you will wake up and not want to follow through on the activities you will commit to while reading this book. I have seen it time and again: people have chosen a goal, set the roadmap, and followed the plan for a while before losing interest, faith, or both and stopping short of their goal. It's often the breakdown just before the breakthrough.

You must clearly understand why you are getting out of bed every day and following your plan, especially on the days when you don't feel like it. Think about how your decision today will impact your future. How about the future of your business? How about your clients? Or, more importantly, what about your family's future?

If you are crystal clear about why you want to work hard to build a real estate business and create this level of income, then you will push through on even the most trying days. When you lack clarity around your goals and your plan, then you will likely flounder and fall short of your goals.

How would your life change if you were to earn $100,000 next year? What would you use the money for? What new choices and options would become available? Whether your goal is making $200,000, $500,000, or several million, the exercise remains the same. You must answer the question: why am I willing to work to earn $500,000 this year? What about that money is important? How will it affect my life, my business, and my family? How will I spend, invest, or contribute? What impact can I make?

Until we learn to pull that pleasure close to us and blind ourselves to the pain of stepping outside of our comfort zone, we will continue to fall short of our potential. When we have clarity in purpose behind our activities, then nothing can stop us from achieving our goals.

You may have pitfalls. You may get off track. You may have to adjust your timeline. However, if we develop a clear understanding of what we are going after and why, build a plan we know will work, and implement at a high level, we cannot fail. Are you willing to commit?

Chapter 2

DAILY SUCCESS RITUALS

Having a routine eliminates the need to avoid pain on a daily basis. Building habits stops the discussion around whether or not you will do something. We don't think about brushing our teeth every day. We have conditioned ourselves that it is just something we do. There is no need for a battle of willpower to force ourselves to brush our teeth. We don't negotiate over things we either do every day or things we know we would never do.

We only have so much energy for making decisions. Finding the willpower to complete the tasks we know we need to do to grow our business requires our energy. There will be parts of growing the business you will not love. We need to get over it and move on. The question is whether you will endure the trials and difficulties of growing your business. This battle is won in the heart and mind. Commit to your goal, use the strategies in this book, and set yourself up for success with your daily success rituals.

It Starts in the Morning

It is not a big surprise that a co-author of a book called *The Miracle Morning for Salespeople* will yell and scream about how important your morning is to the rest of your day. My life underwent a cosmic shift for the better in the year I started practicing The Miracle Morning routine, thanks to my friend, mentor, and co-author Hal Elrod. If you haven't read his book yet, you should go buy it and implement the teachings immediately. If not for your business, then for the benefits of your life, family, friends, health, and every other aspect that practicing the morning routine will impact.

Hal will be the first one to tell you he teaches nothing new in this book. These strategies and tools have been around for thousands of years. The beauty of Hal's book and morning routine is in the simplicity. It's easy to implement. Most people have heard of these techniques before reading the book, yet they have never implemented them before, or at least not all of them.

Hal teaches the principles of the Life S.A.V.E.R.S., a simple acronym for the six daily success rituals that will improve your life, your energy, and your business. Success in real estate sales will require mental, physical, and emotional energy you will generate each day through your success ritual.

The S.A.V.E.R.S.

The daily S.A.V.E.R.S. include:

- **Silence**—This could be meditation, deep breathing, or prayer. Just give your mind a chance to take a break. Recognize the pattern of constant thought and take control.
- **Affirmations**—We create our own story in our subconscious mind. Affirmations are your way to shift the story. I teach an

exercise in one of my classes, which I borrowed from someone else to whom I would give credit if I could remember where it came from.

The exercise requires people to write the five worst things they have ever said about themselves. Then they have to circle the worst one, partner up, and call their partner those horrible names. Lazy. Good for nothing. Stupid. Etcetera, etcetera. It's extremely uncomfortable. These are words you would never say about someone else, but yet they are part of the story we tell or think about ourselves. Affirmations help us shift that story so we don't buy into the bogus bullshit story about how we aren't good enough, worthy enough, strong enough, smart enough, good-looking enough, or whatever particular hang-up you have created that gets in your way.

- **Visualization**—This is the opportunity to cement your new beliefs and see them unfold in your mind before they happen, so we are mentally prepared. Visualization is the preview of coming attractions. This is your opportunity to change the ending.

One person we interviewed for the book discussed how they use their shower time each morning to visualize their most important meeting of the day. They speak the words and responses out loud because it always sounds better in their head than when they say it. This gives them the chance to improve. Imagine the shift in confidence walking into that meeting, knowing what you will say and that it sounds great.

- **Exercise**—This is not just about getting your blood flowing, waking yourself up, creating energy and momentum, and maintaining health. Your energy is vital to being persuasive in sales. Your energy is contagious and will impact your prospects, clients, and team as you grow your business.

- **Reading**—Always do what you can to learn new things. You are reading this book to gain knowledge and perspective in growing a successful real estate business. We will offer you additional tools, podcasts, websites, and coaching programs from different people, trainers, and companies for you to continue your learning. The reason for this book is to introduce you to all the possibilities and options for growing your business so you can find the handful that resonate with how you want to build your business. Each day, you should seek to continue to add to that knowledge and become a master in a few different areas.

- **Scribing**—Scribing is just a fancy word for writing or journaling that makes the S.A.V.E.R.S. acronym work. This is an opportunity for you to write about your successes, record any valuable lessons you've learned, and gain clarity.

Habit Stacking and Scaffolding for Explosive Growth

"Your level of success will seldom exceed your level of personal development, because success is something you attract by the person you become."—Jim Rohn

This morning success ritual is only the beginning of how these new habits will help you build a successful business. Even in the morning routine, we teach people to build on smaller and simpler habits you already do every day. Adding one more habit or system to one you already have in place is easier than trying to start from scratch. Start with something as simple as brushing your teeth, drinking a glass of water, or making your bed.

Stacking these habits one after the other will create a pattern or routine you will no longer need to think about. After you create the habit, willpower is no longer required to continue the pattern. It just becomes something you do. Gary Keller and Jay Papasan cover this in detail in *The One Thing*; worth checking out if you haven't read it.

What you believe about how long it takes to build a habit—whether it's 30 days, 40 days, or 66 days—is not nearly as important as your decision to stick it out with focus for the time required to create the habit. Once this habit takes hold, you can add another and then another. Eventually, your whole morning before noon may become part of your routine. Establishing this level of automaticity will ensure that you complete your most important tasks every day to help you grow personally as well as grow your business.

Each lead generation chapter will suggest daily success rituals for that strategy. We will suggest simple ideas that will create explosive results when implemented consistently over time. This form of habit stacking takes time and commitment, but you will see rapid growth in as little as six months or a year when you commit.

To generate a six-figure income, we need to have a six-figure calendar. Time blocking the right activities is essential to your success in this business. We know that things will come up during your transactions that require your attention. Clients will call with concerns or complaints. The appraisal will not come in when you expected, and you may spend the day making additional calls and sending emails to keep the deal together. Here's the thing: we already know this will happen, so we need to account for it in our plan. Expect the unexpected.

By building a calendar of your most lucrative dollar-producing activities first thing in the morning, following your daily personal success rituals, you will watch your business rise to new levels. After practicing your daily personal success rituals each morning, you will bring a whole new level of energy to your daily business success rituals.

Imagine making your most important prospecting calls immediately after spending the morning reviewing your goals, writing about what makes you grateful, exercising, and learning a new script. Consider how that may impact those first few conversations of the day. Getting these first few calls and lead generation activities completed in the morning not only provides us with the best energy for the greatest impact but also gives people the whole day to call or email you back, and it frees up the rest of your day to show homes and negotiate deals knowing your business development needs were handled first thing in the morning. That's empowering.

This simple practice will help you create a steady flow of business and income. When you stabilize your business and income, you will not be as concerned with when your next commission will arrive. You will make better decisions for your clients. You will exude confidence. All of this will only fuel your business to grow faster. As your business grows, your goals will expand and, most importantly, you will grow each day into a stronger person. This morning routine will help set you up for success in all areas of your life.

That's what this book is really about: building the lifestyle you want for yourself. Real estate is your career. It's not who you are. This is your vehicle to create income and impact people. You are in an excellent position to help people with one of the most important decisions they will make in their life: buying their home. Real estate sales also offers you an unlimited income potential to build a business that can fund the life of your dreams. That life starts with these simple habits.

Think about how a schedule as simple as this might help you break through to earning a multiple six-figure income. Following is an example of someone who focused their lead generation in three areas, including sphere of influence and past clients, working with investors, and contacting For Sale By Owners to list their property. Your schedule may look different from this, based on your plan. You might never call a FSBO. You may not work with investors. You may focus on writing quality content on your website to develop

SEO traffic for generating online leads. Regardless of what the right activities are for your business model, accomplishing them in the morning will guarantee they get done and create results.

MONDAY	
6:00 - 7:00 A.M.	Morning Routine
7:00 – 8:00 A.M.	You/Family Time
8:00 - 8:30 A.M.	Affirmations and Script Practice
8:30 – 9:30 A.M.	Talk to 10 Spheres of Influence / Past Clients
9:30 – 10:00 A.M.	Send 5 Handwritten Notes and 5 Private Facebook Messages
10:00 – 11:00 A.M.	Coffee with 2 Prospects / Ambassadors
11:00 – 12:00 P.M.	Email and Voicemail—Read and Respond
TUESDAY	
6:00 - 7:00 A.M.	Morning Routine
7:00 – 8:00 A.M.	You/Family Time
8:00 - 8:30 A.M.	Affirmations and Script Practice
8:30 – 9:30 A.M.	Call 10 FSBOs
9:30 – 10:00 A.M.	Send 10 Handwritten Notes to FSBOs
10:00 – 11:00 A.M.	Coffee with 2 Prospects / Ambassadors
11:00 – 12:00 P.M.	Email and Voicemail—Read and Respond
WEDNESDAY	
6:00 - 7:00 A.M.	Morning Routine
7:00 – 8:00 A.M.	You/Family Time

8:00 - 8:30 A.M.	Affirmations and Script Practice
8:30 – 9:30 A.M.	Call 10 Investor Prospects and Send Deals
9:30 – 10:00 A.M.	Send 5 Handwritten Notes and 5 Private Facebook Messages to Investors
10:00 – 11:00 A.M.	Coffee with 2 Prospects / Ambassadors
11:00 – 12:00 P.M.	Email and Voicemail—Read and Respond
THURSDAY	
6:00 - 7:00 A.M.	Morning Routine
7:00 – 8:00 A.M.	You/Family Time
8:00 - 8:30 A.M.	Affirmations and Script Practice
8:30 – 9:30 A.M.	Talk to 10 Spheres of Influence / Past Clients
9:30 – 10:00 A.M.	Send 5 Handwritten Notes and 5 Private Facebook Messages
10:00 – 11:00 A.M.	Coffee with 2 Prospects / Ambassadors
11:00 – 12:00 P.M.	Email and Voicemail—Read and Respond
FRIDAY	
6:00 - 7:00 A.M.	Morning Routine
7:00 – 8:00 A.M.	You/Family Time
8:00 - 8:30 A.M.	Affirmations and Script Practice
8:30 – 9:30 A.M.	Talk to 10 Spheres of Influence / Past Clients
9:30 – 10:00 A.M.	Send 5 Handwritten Notes and 5 Private Facebook Messages

10:00 – 11:00 A.M.	Coffee with 2 Prospects / Ambassadors
11:00 – 12:00 P.M.	Email and Voicemail—Read and Respond
SATURDAY	
OFF or showing property depending on leverage and clients.	
SUNDAY	
OFF or showings or open houses depending on leverage and clients.	

You may be surprised to see the suggestion of both weekend days off in a book about selling real estate. Not all real estate businesses require a ton of hours on the weekend. It depends on your clients, the expectations you establish upfront, and your ability to find quality staff to leverage your time. This may take a while to achieve, but certain clients do not require nights and weekends. For instance, if much of the business focuses on investors, weekdays may work just fine for showings.

Regardless of the schedule you determine best fits your needs, you must communicate your expectations and your methods with your clients up front. When you establish clear expectations, you always have the ability to over-deliver. The most important thing is to complete all your lead generation activities in the morning, leaving your afternoons free to handle any client management or issues. This will guarantee a successful day regardless of what happens in the afternoon. If you are always working on finding new business in the morning, you will be less concerned and distracted if something should fall apart in the afternoon.

Developing these daily habits of business building and lead generation will ensure steady growth in your business and income. This steady growth will lead to the opportunity to add leverage and free your schedule further. This freedom will allow you to improve your lifestyle, take more time off, travel, or do other things that are important to you, all while your business continues to grow. It will free you up to spend more time on these daily success rituals that will continue your personal and professional growth.

Chapter 3

GROW YOUR DATABASE

Befo re we get into how to grow your database, you may won-
der if there's a "magic number" to shoot for. Should you keep
your database smaller and more intimate or cast a wide net in
the hope of gathering huge numbers? There are arguments on both
sides for whether you should have a few hundred relationships in
your database you foster at a high level or if you should have tens
of thousands you consistently drip your message to automatically,
turning your business into a pure numbers game. What I have not
heard argued is whether or not you need to grow a database to grow
your business; that's a given. Your network is your net worth. You can
decide if your database should be based on quality or quantity based
both on your personal preference and the lead generation plan you
develop for your business.

Regardless of whether you focus on only a couple hundred people with whom you maintain high-quality relationships—including
gifts, handwritten notes, phone calls, and face time—or if you have
emails segmented for different groups based on tens of thousands

of emails you have collected through online campaigns, you must have a system. A database is not just a list of names, phone numbers, emails, and mailing addresses. While all of that information is vital to staying in touch with people because it allows us to communicate in several forms of media, the information on its own will not grow your business.

Relationships will grow your business. The people in your database are the people we are looking to build relationships with so we might help them or their friends, family, and co-workers with their real estate needs in the future. Our ability to stay in touch with people and consistently seek to provide value will aid us in building these relationships. That is the power of the database. The database should include not only contact information but also notes about our interactions and reminders for timely follow-up. Let's face it, we are always busy in real estate, and dropping the ball with a potential client could cost us thousands if not tens of thousands of current business and potentially hundreds of thousands in future business if they would have turned into one of our top referral sources. This is just not something we should leave to chance.

When choosing a customer relationship management (CRM) system to maintain your database, there is no shortage of options. Since the options are ever- changing, you can find a free break-down of many of the top choices, the features they offer, and their pricing structure on our website at www.explosivesalesgrowth.com/realestate.

In this chapter, we will discuss the features you may consider and the role that each will play in helping you grow your business. Just like with any of the tools we discuss in the book, there is no right or wrong tool. There is only a right or wrong tool for your business based on what you need to do with it. If you are unsure where to even start, then don't get bogged down in the features and just choose an easy system you can quickly implement. The best systems in the world are the ones you will actually implement. That being said, please make sure you can easily import and export data with whatever CRM you choose. This way, you can change or upgrade more easily in the future.

Let's look at some features we should consider in order to utilize our CRM at the highest level to grow relationships and our business.

Contact Management

The ability to import and export leads is an important feature. The goal of the CRM is to save you time and make you more efficient in contacting your prospects. Wasting time manually entering leads into a system or multiple systems will not improve efficiency or productivity. Make sure your CRM will accept lead imports automatically from your third-party lead sources like Zillow, Trulia, Realtor, Facebook, etc. This should not be a problem with most CRM/database systems at this point. Lastly, make sure you can export all content easily as we mentioned earlier; that way, if you decide at some point that you need a more robust system, you can take your data with you.

Ensure that you can easily manage lead sources by being able to tag or group clients. This will ensure that you can send useful content to your prospects and clients based on groups they fall under or tags you have assigned. It will make searching for specific types of clients easier, and you can send new listing information to prospects who have viewed similar properties in the past.

Time Management

Reminders are a key component to managing your database. Setting follow-up reminders after conversations with prospects will ensure that your longer-term pipeline prospects do not fall through the cracks. Implementing this feature is priceless. Make sure the reminders show up in a place where you will see them daily so you remember to follow up. This calendar and task management system could earn you tens of thousands in commissions that get converted instead of falling through the cracks. It will also save you time by not having to leave the system to write in your calendar software.

Automation will be one of your additional time savers. Though some contact management systems will require an extensive set-up to automate texts and emails to potential clients, the payoff over thousands of leads with improved lead conversion and speed to lead will far outweigh the set-up time or cost. This is one of those areas where paying someone else to do the work or buying a more robust system with the automation built in may be worth the investment. It all depends on what you need from your system to support your business and how tech-savvy you are.

Communication Log

If you want people to know you care about them, then it's important that you listen to what they have to say. In order for them to feel as though you listen to and care about them, you actually have to remember your last conversation. When your database only has a handful of people in it that may be simple. However, when you reach the point of having thousands (or tens of thousands if you use online marketing) of leads, keeping a record of their unique wants and needs is of the utmost importance. Whether the system tracks by text, email, notes, or calls, keeping notes on your conversations to reference in future contacts will improve your conversion. It's important that your clients and prospects do not feel like they are just one of many.

Several CRMs will sync with your email at this point and keep track of what people open and click on. This will not only remind you of your last conversation, but it can provide useful information about what media or information resonates with this prospect. The more advanced systems will even let you automate the next step based on what they opened or clicked. This intelligent automation will help to offer value and convert more of your prospects.

Even simple drip campaigns, a set of email content that automatically is delivered over time, can ensure that you have several more touches with your prospects. While email is not the most effective form of communication, since people are inundated with emails, it is far better than no communication at all. In many cases, you may not have any other options when leads register on Facebook with only their email information or if someone provides an incorrect phone number. The more personalized we can be with our communications, the better, but sometimes automated is better than none.

Calling and Texting within your CRM

This feature is available in many of the CRM software options now, and it will save you tons of time. Being able to text or call from within the software will stop you from having to leave the software to communicate with prospects. It also tracks the text messages and responses right in the prospect or client's file, allowing you to keep great notes on the conversations you have had. Most of the CRM's that offer this feature will also track this activity and measure responses.

With many available features, you will need to decide how important each is to your business. I love having all my tools in one place and cannot imagine living without this capability now that I have experienced it, but you may find it is not as important to you. Some agents prefer to keep things separate for organization purposes. You will have to make some decisions based on your own needs and wants.

Video Functionality

We are a visual species, especially in this information age. Video provides a medium to get your message and branding across in a short time period. If a picture is worth a thousand words, well let's just say that a video is thirty pictures per second.

You get the idea. There is power in video. Look at the rise of things like YouTube and Facebook Live. (Those names are relevant at the time of this writing, though with how quickly things evolve online, I am sure I will be replacing them in a future version. For instance, I met my wife on MySpace. Remember when that was a thing?)

You will find different options for interacting via video. Some CRMs will offer video texting or messaging. Others will offer integration through a third-party tool like BombBomb. You will need to decide if video is a functionality you will use to build relationships. Consider the personal touch of being able to see someone speaking directly to you. Consider the recognition. What if you branded your videos, so your logo was visible in the bottom corner of the screen? If the goal is to stay top of mind, then video will surely support that objective.

Deal and Pipeline Management

This feature goes beyond just managing your relationships. This steps outside the role of the CRM. Deal and pipeline management are technically more project management system features. Keep in mind, though, that we want to track our return on investment (ROI). While it is not a requirement for a powerful CRM to track your deals, I find that the ability to do so makes it easier to keep track of which leads and lead sources are providing the most business. It also allows me to quickly compare which messaging, timing, and media seem to attract the most clients that close. Measuring your conversion is the key to determining your current ROI and improving it in the future. However, you may already have a system in place for that, like a simple spreadsheet or a third-party system you love.

Bottom line is that a feature-rich system is great if you intend to use all the bells and whistles. If not, it may clutter your workspace and cause you to use the entire CRM less frequently if it seems too complicated. It also may impact your budget substantially as you get further into an all-in-one system.

You will need to decide what works best for your business. And the system that works best for most businesses is the one that you will actually use regularly.

Document Management

Technology in document management has become a huge time-saver and created a tremendous improvement in productivity. Systems like DocuSign and Dotloop have made it easier to complete transactional paperwork and maintain it safely for future access.

Warning: Please do not let technological advances lower the level of service you provide to your clients. Certain contracts and forms require explaining and potentially a question and answer (Q&A) session in order for your client to feel confident and comfortable. Just because you can send a document for a signature via email doesn't always mean you should. Consider your audience and help them based on their needs. Some people will think digital documents are the greatest invention ever, and others will hate it.

As far as connecting digital documents to your CRM, once again you will need to decide if this is a feature that must be included. I know several agents who successfully manage a separate system for documents and checklists for their active clients. Others swear by keeping everything in one place. Some of these CRMs will work with third-party software for this capability.

Be careful, as some of these third-party connections can be clunky at the time of this writing; with that being said, many of these solutions tend to improve quite rapidly. You should, however, always seek your broker approval when connecting any broker forms or docs to your own system.

Staying Ahead of the Curve

For an up-to-date analysis of available products and pricing with a breakdown of features for each product, please visit our web site at: **www.explosivesalesgrowth.com/realestate**.

Chapter 4

KNOW YOUR MARKET

W e don't sell houses. We sell our service of helping somebody find and buy the right house or sell their current home; making the process simple and painless; helping them to negotiate a fair price and terms; and effectively marketing a home when selling. To provide a high level of service both in buying and selling, we must have an intimate understanding of the market in which we are building our business.

You should plan to look daily at the MLS in your area to study what is happening in the local market. You should have a deep understanding of pricing and how to find comparable sales in order to create an accurate comparative market analysis (CMA). This is an integral part of pricing on the listing side of the business and in getting offers accepted on the buying side.

Especially as a new agent, I studied the market in my area each day. I would look at new listings as they came on the market. I would look at what was pending each week to see what types of homes and price ranges were selling. I studied average days on market. I also studied what wasn't selling. The homes that did not sell offered clues as to what I needed to avoid. They also offered examples for my listing clients when I needed to explain the importance of staging, professional photographs, or even the dangers of over-pricing their home. I quickly learned the neighborhoods where I planned to focus my business.

Don't Spread Yourself Too Thin

The tendency of most agents when they do not have as much business as they would like is to run all over the place showing homes to buyers well outside of their comfort zone. Some agents would say this is a disservice to the client although I do not necessarily agree with that. Having a great agent from a different town does not make a client worse off than having a mediocre or lackluster agent from the town where they are purchasing a home. I would argue, though, that it is not always in your best interest to take on clients outside your area of expertise.

Now, if it's your first client, you could argue that you don't yet have an area of expertise, and maybe this commission check allows you to stay in the business long enough to figure it all out. I wouldn't really argue with either of those points. Soon there will come a time when it makes more sense to refer business to another agent. You will have to decide that distance based on your business and your location. In some areas, driving a half hour to a showing may be perfectly normal; whereas in a metro area, leaving your three-block radius may be too far.

The benefits of working a certain area are plentiful. You will build brand recognition much faster in a contained area like a town or a neighborhood than if you sell homes throughout an entire county. In many of the towns near me, ten or twelve transactions per year would put you in the top five to ten agents for the town. In other areas, you would need fifty closings to hit the top few agents. You will need to decide what is best for your location.

You will also save time when you do not have to travel more than ten to fifteen minutes between appointments. Consider the mileage on your car as well. And when you show houses or list properties in areas where you do not want to generate leads, that is time not spent prospecting or generating leads in your primary locations.

You will also gain intense knowledge in pricing and negotiating when you are listing and buying several homes in the same location. Spreading yourself too thin will make it more difficult to become the area expert in your market.

Find Your Niche

Specialists get paid more. Again, in the beginning it may take time to find the niche in which you are passionate, have a natural talent, or just happen to know a lot of people. Look for overlap. You may find it is as simple as working a particular neighborhood or town like we discussed, but not all niches are geographic.

You may find you have a special skill set that makes you stand out in working with people who are downsizing. Maybe you love helping them through the emotional component of leaving the home where they may have raised their family. You might have a way of helping them understand how staging and some repairs may help their home sell for more money.

Some of you may dislike working with those clients; emotions are not your strong suit. You would rather have the excitement of helping first-time homebuyers and teaching them the process. Maybe you love crunching numbers and looking for potential investment properties. You may have a focus on investor clients.

Regardless of your niche, landing your preferred prospects as clients will become easier and more lucrative when they know you are the expert. People want to work with people they know, like, and trust. Being the expert will make people trust you a lot faster when you can show them how you have helped others in their position.

Get into the Homes

Knowing the market through researching everything that unfolds in MLS is helpful as far as having knowledge and a reference point for what is going on out there. Getting into the homes and seeing the layout, the condition, the location, and the details of the property will make you far more resourceful.

When an online lead calls and says, "I am interested in 125 Maple Street," you have a huge advantage if you have been in the home.

Consider the following conversation:

> **Agent:** "Great, can you tell me what you like about it based on what you have seen online?"
>
> **Prospect:** "Well, it has three bedrooms and looks like the kitchen and baths have been updated."
>
> **Agent:** "You know what, I was in 125 Maple Street the other day, and you are right about the kitchen. I can see why you would like it. Quick question: what else is really important to you in finding a home? What are your top five must-haves?"
>
> **Prospect:** "We would like three beds, two baths, a nice kitchen, updated main systems since we don't want to spend a lot of money right after we buy, and quiet neighborhood."
>
> **Agent:** "Very nice. It sounds like you have put a lot of thought into what you need. I am happy to show you the property.

Based on what you told me, there are two things you should know. The heating system looks older, which could need replacing and that's something we could ask for at home inspection. The one thing we can't change is that even though it's in a neighborhood, it lands right at the end of the street, so it's on the corner of the neighborhood and the main road. Not sure if that would be a deal-breaker for you or not."

Prospect: "Thanks for all the information. This was helpful. I think we would still look at it if you think we may negotiate with them to upgrade the heating system."

Agent: "Great. Here's my suggestion. How about if we meet at my office first and talk a little more about what you like and don't like? We can look at some homes together online and narrow down your search so I can save you a bunch of time and aggravation. Then we can head right over to look at 125 Maple. How does that sound?"

Prospect: "Sounds great."

Agent: "Perfect. I can meet tomorrow at 10 A.M. or 2 P.M. Which one works better for you?"

You gain a ton of credibility with online leads when you have been in the homes they are calling about. They could make assumptions about you as an agent, including that you are knowledgeable, active in the market, and have access to information they can't gather from an online search.

That's it. That's the big one right there. Information is easy to access online these days. Years ago, agents were the gatekeepers of the listing information. People would have to walk into a real estate office to find out what was on the market. You just had to sit there and wait. That's not true anymore. Now, we have to distinguish ourselves from the rest of the market. Having an expert level of market knowledge in a particular niche will make you stand out, and people will be more likely to refer you because they know how much value you will bring to the table for their friends, family, and co-workers.

Be Faster and More Personable than the Internet

One way to show your clients you stay ahead of what's happening on the market is to alert your buyers of a great new property that meets their needs or your sellers of a new listing competing with their home. Technology makes this easy for us in most cases. There is nothing wrong with automatically sending clients homes that meet their criteria through a listing alert, but I would not stop there.

The relationship matters. You don't build relationships through automated emails. Instead, create a hot sheet for yourself, and check it a couple times per day. Call your clients when the right house pops up. They will know you are working for them all the time to find their dream home.

Or build a hot sheet for any homes that may come on the market that are in direct competition with your listing. You are the agent. You should know the market before the client. This is also an easy thing to leverage to an assistant. Have them check all the hot sheets and let you know of any calls you need to make in the morning or the afternoon.

Show, Don't Tell

When it comes to being the market expert, people are not going to just trust you know what you are talking about when they first meet you. You may know full well that your listing client wants an unreasonable price for their home, and you could try to explain it to them based on your knowledge. Sometimes that may even work, but sometimes, you may find that the client does not agree. They see it as your opinion, and they have a different opinion.

For this reason, I am a firm believer in the concept of showing instead of telling. While they may argue with your explanation, it is much more difficult to argue with fact. Whether I am explaining price to a potential seller or trying to help a buyer formulate a winning offer, it always starts with comparable sales (or "comps"). You need to have a firm understanding of pricing to be seen as a market expert. When you show someone three or four homes that have sold in the past three to six months that look just like their home, questioning the value becomes a lot more difficult.

If they still disagree with the price, ask questions based in fact rather than emotion; people may take offense to their home not being as good as they thought. Ask questions like, "What about your home is different?"

Script:

My goal is to sell your home for as much money as we can to help you get the home of your dreams. We are both better off in that case. I want you to be so happy with the service we provide that you would refer all of your family and friends to me.

I just don't want to tell you I can sell your home for more than what the market will allow, because then you will not only be disappointed in me, but you won't achieve your goal of buying a new home.

The real estate market works like other markets. It is based on the law of supply and demand. While we cannot affect supply since we cannot ask people in town to keep their homes off the market while we list your home, we can affect demand. We want to make sure your home is the nicest home in the

---

market for the best price in its price range. That way, everyone searching in that price range will want to see *your* home.

What do you think will happen if everyone searching for a home in your price range wants to see *your* home?

Exactly. We would expect to receive offers because people do not want to miss out on your home that everyone wants to buy. Having offers allows us to negotiate from a point of strength. Sitting on the market makes us negotiate from a point of weakness. Would you rather come from a point of weakness or strength?

Strength. Right. So, after looking at what other similar homes are selling for and what is on the market now, what price do you think allows us to negotiate from a point of strength?

Know the Neighborhoods

Real estate is a local business. Understanding the market means understanding the differences in neighborhoods. While we do not want to steer buyers toward or away from neighborhoods, it is important that we understand how neighborhoods impact value.

I live in a small town. There are only approximately 1500 homes in my town, and several of them are oceanfront or close to the Atlantic Ocean, so location impacts values. While refinancing my home, the bank sent an appraiser who was not from the area to appraise my home, and because of the low number of comparable sales available, they pulled comps from a neighboring town. It's a fairly common practice where I live.

Unfortunately, not being from the area, they did not understand the difference between my small town and a much larger neighboring town with a high tourism volume. The values are much lower in the neighboring town. Had they looked north and west of us to two other neighboring towns, they would have found similar populations, school rankings, and housing markets.

We had to order a second appraisal to get an accurate value of our home. Had this been a real estate agent, we would not have hired them. They would have valued our home at nearly $75,000 under its actual value because they did not understand the local market.

You need not be from the area where you sell real estate, you need to have an in-depth knowledge of the market that comes from viewing homes online and in person and watching the market consistently. Agents looking to explode their sales volume browse their MLS and view homes to stay ahead of the market movement to provide the highest level of service to their clients.

KNOW YOUR MARKET SUCCESS RITUALS

Daily:

- Check hot sheets each morning for listing and buyer clients and call them to discuss important market changes before that information shows up in their email.

Weekly:

- Let clients know about price changes, expired homes, and new listings that affect their search or the pricing of their listing.

- View open houses of new listings. Touring homes will give you the best information available in the market.

Monthly/Quarterly:

- Write a blog or newsletter about your local market.

Chapter 5

IT STARTS WITH YOUR SPHERE

H aving trained hundreds of real estate agents, I have seen the discomfort in their eyes when I let them know that reaching out to family, friends, past schoolmates and co-workers will likely be their number one source of business when they first get started.

There are several reasons your sphere of influence will likely be the people to propel you forward into a successful real estate career, including:

- Most agents generate sixty to seventy percent of their business from their sphere of influence, including past clients and referrals (including agents who have been successful for years).

- Your friends and family already know, like, and trust you, which is an important element in getting anyone to want to do business with you.

- Talking to your friends and family is something that will come naturally, so you can practice "selling" without the pressure of meeting with complete strangers.

- People like to talk about real estate, so finding opportunities to bring it up in everyday conversations without being obnoxious will be simple.

- Of the hundreds of people you likely know, we only need ten to twenty of them to either buy or sell a home or refer business to you to kick off a successful business.

Build Your Database

The difference between just talking to friends and family and lead generating for your business is all about being purposeful. Being purposeful starts with a database of contacts from which you can actively generate leads. The database is a living, breathing, ever-changing organism. This is not just a list of names, emails and phone numbers. The database is a location to manage contact info, keep track of conversations, set follow-up reminders and appointments, and group your contacts so you can market and prospect effectively.

There are several options for choosing a database though it's likely your brokerage will provide one for you. Which database you choose is not as important in the beginning of your career as actually using one. In fact, simple may be better in the beginning. Some options out there include Market Leader's eEdge, Realty Juggler, Top Producer, Real Geeks, Brivity, LionDesk, Contactually, Happy Grasshopper, and Follow-Up Boss. I am sure there will be many more to surface over the years. The key is to understand what you need your database to do, and then choose the one you are most likely to learn and use.

Gathering Contact Information

Once you have chosen your database solution, you must input your contacts into your database. You can prepare this in advance by creating a spreadsheet with columns for first name, last name, street address, city, state, zip code, email, and phone number. These pieces of information are important, since we want to stay in touch with our sphere in lots of different ways, including email, snail mail, phone calls, instant messaging, and face-to-face meetings.

Pro Tip: Don't let building your database be the reason you have not started calling people, especially if you have a large number of contacts to import. Reach out to people as you enter them in the database. If you have their phone number but not their email or street address, you can ask for the missing information during your phone conversation. If you do not have their phone number, you can shoot them a quick email or instant message (through Facebook) and let them know you wanted to call but realized you did not have their number in your new phone. Watch how fast you gather information! Then, once they send it, you have to actually call. Your real estate business will grow in proportion to the number of real estate conversations you are having.

What If My Friends Aren't Buying or Selling Homes?

Here's the thing: only one in ten people are likely to buy or sell a home this year. Even if someone in your network isn't the one, they likely know more than ten people you do not know. Think about their co-workers, church groups, kids' sports or other activities; they are connected to hundreds of people you likely don't know. Some of our sphere will champion our names in front of others and drive referral business to us. It only takes a handful of those people to build a successful real estate business.

Michael Maher talks about Dunbar's Number in his book, *7L: The Seven Levels of Communication: Go from Relationships to Referrals*. Dunbar's Number states we can maintain strong relationships with approximately 150 people. That's exciting news if the need to have thousands of people in your database concerned you. Maintaining 150 relationships should lead you to 15 transactions if our 1-in-10 theory is correct. If it's 1 in 7, then you have a better chance of completing 20 transactions. We haven't even discussed that those 20 may sell and then buy as well, which would get you to 40 transactions.

This doesn't take into account that each of your top 150 contacts also know 150 people, which means with one degree of separation, you can connect with 22,500. If 1 in 10 buys a home, you have 2,250 transactions and if they sell and buy, we are looking at 4,500.

The average commission in our office is $8,750. With that in mind, there is over $39 million in potential commissions sitting one degree away from you right now. Are you starting to understand the importance of building and contacting your database?

The key is that we need to develop the conversations in such a way that it makes sense to reach out to people who are not buying and selling this year. We concede that 90 percent of them will not be in the market this year. We still need to stay top of mind with them if we will generate a high level of referral business from our sphere of influence.

What Are We Supposed to Say When We Call?

If we consistently just call to ask for business, we will have people dodging our calls and deleting our emails. We want to build relationships and connections in our database. Asking somebody every month if they want to sell their house is not likely to earn us many friends if we aren't providing them value.

I want to offer you some specific examples of conversations you can have with your sphere that will lead to real estate conversations without constantly calling and asking them for something. Keep in mind you will find countless ways to have these types of conversations. The key is just to stay in contact.

Always Provide Value

If I asked you for something every time I reached out to you, you may get sick of hearing from me. However, if I offered you something valuable every time we spoke, you would look forward to my call. We can provide value in two simple ways: our relationships and our market knowledge.

A simple way to reach out to your sphere of influence is to check for recently sold or just listed properties in their neighborhood. For many people, their real estate is their greatest investment, and their equity may be the largest portion of their net worth. That being said, most people are interested in the value of their home regardless of whether they are considering buying or selling at the moment. The market value of their own home is based on comparable sales, or the sales of other homes in their neighborhood similar to their home. That's why being knowledgeable about the market allows us to provide value.

Sample Script

Agent: "Hey (Friend/Homeowner Name). It's (Your Name). How are you?"

Homeowner: "We're good. How are you?"

Agent: "Great. I was just calling to share some information you might find interesting. Do you have a couple minutes?"

Homeowner: "Sure."

Agent: "Perfect. Well, I like to stay on top of the market, so I can offer value to my clients in pricing and negotiating. In the process of checking out the recently sold properties, I noticed that 28 Main Street right down the street from your house sold for $430,000. I know you guys probably aren't thinking about moving right now, but I thought you might be interested to know since it has similar beds and baths as your house."

Homeowner: "Thanks a lot."

Agent: "Hey (Homeowner Name), one last thing. Would you do me a huge favor?"

Homeowner: "Sure."

Agent: "You guys are in a great neighborhood. We always have buyers checking that area out, but sometimes the specific homes available just aren't a fit. If you hear of anyone in your neighborhood even thinking about selling, would you let me know? I would love to get some of our buyers in there."

Homeowner: "Sure."

Agent: "Thanks, (Homeowner Name). I appreciate it. Let us know if you need anything. Talk with you soon."

In this case, we are using sold data relevant to the person in my sphere because it is local to their neighborhood and affects the pricing of their property. It's much more comfortable asking for referrals at the end of the call once I have been able to provide them with information of value. If someone says they do not have a couple of minutes or they sound like there is a lot going on, just ask if there is a better time for you to follow up. Say it sounds like they are busy, and you want to respect their time. If they don't answer, I would leave a message, and let them know you have information about a house that just sold down the street from them that you think might interest them.

You could call and have similar conversations about basic market data, like the change in average sale prices for homes in their area the number of days on market, shifts in interest rates and how they are affecting the market. You could also call and tell them about a property that just listed in their neighborhood, let them know the price, and see if they would be interested in choosing their neighbor. If so, ask if they know anyone who may want to move to their neighborhood whom you can contact about the property.

Your knowledge of the industry and market is tremendously valuable. If you have additional market information you could provide regularly through your emails or an app, then the end of your phone call would be a great time to offer that option. If they enjoyed the call and were happy to receive the market info you offered, then they may say yes to getting your market updates. This would allow you to stay in front of them regularly as well. Remember, the key here is to offer value. The more localized we can make our market updates, the more useful the information will be, and the greater the value to the people receiving them. Also, data is useful, but most people can find data. If you want to provide even greater value, offer your expert explanation and interpretation of the data. That is not something people can get anywhere else except from you.

Providing Value to Your Clients

So far, we have discussed providing value to your prospects regardless of whether you have met them yet. The second part of the equation has to do with your value proposition to your clients. There are likely hundreds, if not thousands, of real estate agents out there your clients could choose to work with. Your value proposition sets you apart from the rest. The best part of having a clear value proposition is that it will separate you from the pack as I have found that few agents have much clarity about what they bring to their clients that is different from what every other agent claims to bring to their clients.

Let's take it a step further now. Living out that value proposition is what is going to create referral business for you. The need for referrals is not unique to real estate sales, but the importance for us is significant because we operate in a slightly different industry. It's not like owning a restaurant or having a cleaning service where clients can return daily, weekly, or monthly. We will still aim to develop repeat clients, but the fact is that the average homeowner only changes homes every seven to ten years, depending on the location.

If I owned a company in most any other industry that relies on repeat business, as in our previous restaurant example, and someone said to me, "Ryan, we absolutely love your company. This is the best service we have ever had. We cannot wait to come back. See you in seven years," that would be a significant issue. In real estate, though, that's the norm. Granted, you may have some investor clients that purchase several homes per year or builders that buy lots and sell whole developments with you; those are both great ways to grow your business, yet they will not be the case for most clients. Most clients will buy one home from you this year and won't come back for seven to ten years.

The most important lesson to take from all of this is that we need to find other ways to generate more business from our clients. If they are not going to become repeat clients for several years, we need to determine how else we can leverage the relationship to help grow our business.

The very first step is creating our value proposition and living it out as we have discussed in the previous paragraphs. What is your unique value proposition to your clients?

Say Referral Again

The next step in generating additional business from your clients is to generate referral business. Referral business is the most profitable form of client ever for several reasons:

- Your referral program will most likely cost you very little in the terms of both money and time invested;

- Your borrowed trust from the initial referring client will make your closing ratio higher;

- You will likely be less at risk of losing to competing agents when it comes to business that you were referred; and

- Referral clients will be likely to refer you to others since the behavior was modeled for them.

Your role is to seek opportunities to talk about referrals throughout the entire process. It doesn't mean that you need to ask for referrals all the time. You just need to talk about them. Here are some examples: When talking about testimonials, you can say things like, "This is what our client, Brian, had to say about working with us. Brian was a referral from Mark and Ellie, who we sold a home to earlier in the year."

In your listing or buyer consult, you can talk about where your business comes from by saying something like, "Over half of our business comes from past clients and referrals. We aim to do such a great job for our clients that they couldn't imagine letting their family, friends, and co-workers work with another agent. They would want their loved ones to have the same great experience that they did. In fact, that's one of the ways we will know we did a great job for you."

Your Relationships Provide Value

I have lived in our home for almost six years, and I still struggle sometimes to find the vendors that I am looking for when I need work completed on my house. Whether it's electricians, plumbers, landscapers, contractors, pest control, etc., your sphere of influence will appreciate your connections to the best vendors in your area. I don't want to get too deep into this topic since there is a whole chapter on this later in the book, but I do want to talk about the sphere side of the relationship here.

This is where we get to create win-win-win relationships. Your sphere wins because they will get reliable service from the top vendors in your network. Your vendors win because you will be consistently referring clients to them. You win because 1) your sphere will find value in your relationships and look to you as a professional for their real estate needs, and 2) the right vendors will refer business to you in return when they come across people who are buying and selling homes. Remember, these vendors are in contact with dozens of people every week. They are likely to come across people who are preparing to sell their homes.

There are two ways to reach out to your sphere when talking about vendors:

1. Call your sphere and ask them for the names of the top vendors that they would recommend to friends or family, those they found to offer only the best, 10+ service. Let them know that you are looking to add to your vendor network to provide great service to your clients.

2. Call your sphere at certain times of the year and offer to provide contact info for a certain vendor they may find useful. Keeping the seasons in mind, you could connect them with a landscaper for spring clean-up or use late fall as a reason to connect them with an HVAC professional to service their heating system. If they already have someone they really like, ask them for that vendor's contact information so you can potentially add them to your vendor network.

This is a great way to provide value while generating new leads for your real estate business. When we come from contribution, people will welcome our calls rather than try to avoid them. When we go out of our way to help our past clients and sphere of influence, they will be far more likely to go out of their way to help us grow our business.

Once You Catch Them, Never Let Them Go

There is an NAR statistic which states that 88% of buyers say they would use their same agent again given the opportunity, yet only 12% actually use the same agent. This statistic is mind-boggling. That means of all the buyers who say they will work with us again—after we work hard to capture them, follow up, find their home, and provide great service right through closing—only a little over one in ten do.

A lot of it comes down to the actions we take. Don't orphan your buyers. Agents are entrepreneurial creatures by nature and are often naturally better at going after the next listing or buyer. Make sure to put systems in place to keep your past clients close. I bought my home six years ago, and I honestly have no idea what my agent's name was. She has never once attempted to stay in touch with us after the closing.

Keep this in mind when you sell a home as the listing agent as well. Don't be afraid to remain a resource for the buyers of your listing. Their agent will likely not stay in touch with them, and you have already proven that you can sell their home.

We spend a lot of time and money finding clients. Once you have won them over, do yourself a favor and hang onto them. They will appreciate being treated like people rather than a transaction.

SPHERE OF INFLUENCE SUCCESS RITUALS

Daily:

- Send 5 text messages or private messages.
- Talk with 5 people about real estate.
- Send 2 handwritten notes.

Weekly:

- Meet with 4 people for coffee, lunch, or dinner.

Monthly/Quarterly:

- Send a mailer (invitation/birthday card/postcard) monthly.
- Send an email monthly.
- Hold a client appreciation event quarterly.

Chapter 6

VENDOR REFERRAL NETWORK

We talked briefly in the last chapter about how you could capitalize on your relationships with professional vendors in the area as a way to provide value to your clients. It creates several opportunities for you to reach out to your sphere of influence and offer them value. Each of these conversations is also a reminder to your friends, family, and clients that you are a real estate professional who services their clients at a high level and that your relationship does not end at the closing table.

Do you think that is the type of agent to whom they would want to refer their friends, family, and co-workers?

The answer to that question should be a resounding "YES!" Think about a time when you have referred someone in the past. My guess is that it was because you felt like that person was truly looking out for your best interest, or because they got you a great deal or provided remarkable service. If you want to build relationships with people who will champion your name as an agent, you must provide that level of value.

Find the Right Vendors

Just as you have high standards for yourself so others may refer you, you should expect the same from any vendors you may refer. Your vendors are an extension of your service, and they should expect to meet or exceed the level of service you would expect for your clients. It's important that you choose the right vendors for your network.

Try to use vendors whose work you or someone you know have seen and respect. In the last chapter, we suggested reaching out to your sphere and past clients and asking them to share any vendors they would consider a 10+ for quality service. This is a great way to connect with your sphere and build a trusted network of vendors.

When you need to find vendors outside of the ones offered by your sphere, we recommend searching online reviews through Yelp, Angie's List, Google, Facebook, etc. There is so much information available online at this point that there is no excuse for not doing a little research. If you have administrative help, this is a perfect project to leverage out to someone else. Remember, these vendors are an extension of your service, so it's vital that we choose great vendors.

Build Vendor Relationships

In reaching out to the vendors, use a simple script to ask them if they have interest in helping to grow each other's business. Let them know you are a real estate agent in the area and are in need of top service providers in their industry. Ask them if they have a real estate agent to whom they refer clients. If they sound open to trading referral business and do not have someone in the real estate industry already in their network, ask them to meet up for coffee, lunch, or a drink after work. If they already refer business to a real estate agent, see if they would be open to considering you as an option. It may be they have always referred to someone who rarely refers back, in which case they may be open to a more mutually beneficial relationship. It could also be their brother or best friend, in which case you may be out of luck, but you won't know until you ask.

When you meet with them, you should use the opportunity to provide value by asking lots of questions about them and their business, such as:

- How long have they been in business?
- What types of specific services do they offer?
- What are their favorite towns or neighborhoods to work in?
- What's one area in which they would like to get more work?
- If you could refer the perfect client who would that be?
- What's the best way to refer business to them?
- Do they have testimonials or past clients that your clients could reach out to for references?

Think about it. If someone asked you these questions about your real estate business, wouldn't you want to have them as a referral partner? As Zig Ziglar said, "In order to get what you want, you just have to help enough other people get what they want."

Grow a Community

At the end of each of your vendor meetings, ask them if they know any other quality professionals in other home-related trades or businesses you should know. If they are a contractor, maybe ask them what plumber or electrician they recommend. You could ask if they have a CPA or financial planner you should speak with. As you build your network, you will have relationships to offer them in return. You can start by referring your vendors to one another.

Once you have established a community, you may find that group meetings make sense, so you can all share in growing one another's businesses. You may bring in outside speakers or meet for breakfast and networking. How you interact is less important than the fact that you develop the network of quality vendors.

The right vendors will make preparing the home for sale and the move itself easier for your clients and should ensure regular referral business. Referral business is the most profitable and typically easiest to close since you can borrow trust from the relationship of your referral partner. Building your referral-based business with vendors will be similar to building it with your sphere. The difference is that vendors often come in contact with a lot more people in the day-to-day operation of running their own businesses. You may find they are more frequently given the opportunity to refer business your way, making your relationships with them even more fruitful and productive.

Make Sure You Add Value to Them

Just like any partnership, the relationship with vendors needs to remain a win-win. Look for opportunities to refer your vendor partners whenever possible. Watch for people asking for recommendations on Facebook. Write online reviews about work they have done for your clients or yourself. Helping your vendors grow their businesses will benefit everyone in the long run when you choose the right vendor relationships.

If vendors understand that you have become a lynchpin in helping their businesses to succeed at a high level, that should transfer to them taking even greater care of your clients. This will reflect even better on your business as well. Always expect to give more than you get in return.

VENDOR NETWORK SUCCESS RITUALS

Daily:

- Look for opportunities to refer prospects and clients to your vendors by asking questions about what they need.
- Talk with two of your vendor partners to stay top of mind.
- Send two handwritten notes.

Weekly:

- Meet with two vendors for coffee, lunch, or dinner.
- Post on social media asking about people's favorite vendors.
- Share your vendors in a book or flyer at each appointment.
- Reach out to three past clients to see if they need anything for their home. With whom can you connect them to add value?

Monthly/Quarterly:

- Thank vendors publicly by sharing success stories on social media.

Chapter 7

LEVERAGING SOCIAL MEDIA

There are many ways to use social media, including advertising, which we will discuss in a couple different chapters in this book. If you could take anything away from this chapter, though, it should be that social media in real estate is as much about what you hear as it is about what you say.

If you read the introduction, I mentioned this in the chapter description. Real estate is a unique market; it is like weddings and children's furniture in that oftentimes, real estate transactions happen based on life events. Sometimes those life events are planned, but often they happen quickly and out of the blue.

People blast their personal lives all over social media, and we have the ability to use that information or data to get in front of people who are more likely to be selling or buying a home soon. While this is true for target marketing through advertising on certain platforms like Facebook, Instagram, or LinkedIn, it also matters when we talk about our sphere of influence.

Interact With Your Sphere of Influence

You cannot spend five minutes on Facebook without finding someone celebrating a life event, whether it's a birthday, engagement, wedding, divorce, new baby, graduation, or new job. Many of these events often trigger someone to consider a change in their living situation. With just a few minutes a day devoted to seeing what is happening in the lives of your extended sphere online, you can gain tremendous insight.

Now, I would not advise jumping from a post that says someone is finalizing their divorce or just gave birth to a new baby—hopefully not both at the same time—to asking them if they need help selling their home and/or finding a new one. It does, however, open the door to a conversation with someone you may not have spoken with in a while. Start with a simple congratulations or condolences, depending on what's appropriate for the scenario. Continue the conversation by coming from a place of curiosity and then from service.

Start by asking questions. How are they doing? How is their family? What else has happened since you last spoke? Get the brief biography. Ask them where they are living now and what they are doing for work. The rule of reciprocity says they will ask you some of the same questions. This should offer you a comfortable opportunity to mention you are in real estate and business has been great. If you have a mutual friend you have already worked with to help find a home, this may be an appropriate time to mention that.

The absolute worst thing that could happen is that you will speak with someone you once knew and then move on. The best-case scenario is that they will be thinking about buying or selling soon or know someone else who is and refer immediate business your way.

What is most likely to happen, though, is something in the middle. You will likely have the opportunity to follow up with future conversations. You may get their address, which will allow you to follow up with a little handwritten note letting them know how much you enjoyed catching up with them and that you look forward to staying in touch.

All we are looking to do is further the relationship and remain top of mind when it comes to their real estate needs. We will never talk someone into buying or selling a home when they have no interest or desire to do so. This is one of my favorite things about real estate sales. There is no need to push. We only need to build and grow relationships and add value in order for people to recognize us as the local expert they would go to for all of their real estate needs when the time arises. Then we need to remain in contact so someone else doesn't take over that spot.

Pro Tip: You can't fake this. You must have an interest in people to make this work at a high level. If you have no desire to talk with people and find out more about what's going on in their lives, then this avenue is not a good one for you. Skip ahead to the online advertising part or another chapter entirely. It's okay if that's what you do. Remember, this book is about introducing the different avenues of growing a real estate business so you can decide the ways that best suit your personality and goals. There is nothing wrong with choosing a different path. In fact, as you may have heard me say earlier in this book, your goal should be to narrow down your top two or three options for lead generation. That means you must eliminate eight or nine of the others.

Develop a Follow-Up Plan

While reaching out after major life events to reignite a relationship and find immediate business is better than not reaching out at all, it will be far more effective with a dedicated follow-up plan. Think back to the steps we talked about in growing your database, and start by getting complete contact information.

I have found that Facebook Messenger is one of the easiest ways to follow up privately with people and get additional contact information.

You might send them a quick message that says, "Hey, I wanted to send you a card to congratulate you. What's your mailing address?" Or, "Drove by your house today and wanted to call but realized I don't have your cell number in my phone."

You will be amazed how quickly you can build up the contact information in your database. This conversation also opens the door for your next touch or conversation. This may seem calculated or cold but remember what I said earlier: you can't fake this part. If you do not sincerely want to build these relationships, you most likely won't end up following through anyways.

Target Your Marketing

Once you build out your contact information in your database and add your notes, you can better target your messaging to the contact based on what would be most helpful to them considering their current situation.

You may break this down based on something as simple as if they currently own a home. You may target them by location to provide relevant market data. Targeting by location can help you incorporate personal stories of clients you helped in the past who may have lived nearby and been just like them.

You may reach these contacts through phone, mail, email, and private messages, but you may also reach them on the same network you rekindled the relationship through. Platforms like Facebook allow you to target specific lists of people with advertising. You can upload a client or prospect list and use that to create a look-a-like audience, targeting folks similar to your database. You can create audiences based on things like age, sex, location, income, employer, or even interests. You have endless opportunities to stay in front of people on social media.

Social Media is Meant to be Social

People come to social media to post about their lives, their family, what they ate for dinner, and to share pictures of vacations, gatherings, concerts, parties, etc. They do not come to social media to be sold to. In fact, people hate being sold to. They love to buy, but they hate to be sold.

With that in mind, it's important to tell your story on social media. Remember that you only need to do two things: continually build the relationship by staying in contact and showcase yourself as the real estate expert in the area. Asking everyone you see on social media if they want to buy or sell a home or posting about your marketing plan is not likely to attract a ton of interaction with people who came there to be social.

Make Sure the Content Matches the Medium

Lengthy, text-heavy messages about the market may not gather a ton of steam in the Facebook arena, while a well-written article about how interest rates are affecting buying power may bode well on LinkedIn. On Facebook, a simple picture celebrating your clients closing on their new home, along with a story or testimonial from them, may get an excellent response, especially if you get your client's permission to tag them or, better yet, they share your post with their friends to increase your audience.

You may spark interest by sharing short videos on Snapchat or Instagram to tell stories or document a quick tour or flash market update.

Advertising on Social Media

At the time of this writing, the most social media advertising dollars were spent on Facebook. You can use this functionality to grow your business in a variety of ways, but there is a cost. Almost everything we have talked about to this point is free or costs little money. Your budget for ad spend can be as little or as much as you see fit, but if you are going to invest, then you should know how to do it well and follow a plan. We will offer several of the basics in this chapter, but we suggest that you check out our resources on our website for mastery if you follow this path: www.explosivesalesgrowth. com/realestate.

The first thing you have to understand is that the point of advertising is two-fold. You can use it to develop brand recognition by catching lots of eyeballs. It may be part of the process of staying in front of your target audience. This works well in a target location with numerous homeowners whom you would like to view your ads. This can be an inexpensive way to help build your brand. When talking with agents who do this well, they frequently hear comments from people like, "I see you everywhere," while they may only have one or two listings.

I would not recommend this as a primary strategy, but it is a great secondary benefit. I am far less likely to focus my lead generation on brand awareness. I would take a much more direct approach in paid advertising. Essentially, I only spend money when it will generate contact information where I can follow up with leads for free. When I focus on brand recognition, I always have to pay to be in front of that prospect. When I shift my focus to lead capture, I can pay to get in front of them again (by running re-targeting ads) or I can call, email, or mail to them if I choose, based on how much information I collect.

Two Requirements of Lead Generation through Advertising

1.) The content has to be more valuable to your lead than their contact information.

This means in order for someone to give permission for you to have their information, whether it's Facebook access, email, phone, address, etc., they must believe they are getting something of equal or greater value. For example, information about a property I could go find on Zillow or Trulia may not be enticing to a savvy individual, but information about a new listing I cannot find anywhere else yet may cause me to give you my email, phone number, or both. A shared article I could just look up on Google may not excite anybody, but a Top 10 List for homes in my town or local area might.

2.) You must have a simple way to capture their information and get them the information they want.

This has become easier and easier for people now with strategies like Facebook Login (which allows people to sign up for your information using their Facebook credentials) and several services you can use to build simple landing pages (also known as capture pages like Lead Pages or Listings-to-Leads). When someone clicks on an ad and lands on a capture page, the capture page should offer simple instructions, like "fill out this form" or "click this button" to get whatever information promised in the ad.

Some examples of ads share simple statistical data about the housing market in a local community that would spark a homeowner's interest and then offering a free home valuation. For example:

San Diego Market Update: The Average Sale Price for a Single Family Home in San Diego has increased 11% this year.

To find out how much equity you have in your home, click here: **www.SanDiegoHomeValues.com.**

Top 10 Condos in Downtown Boston

Check out the area's hottest new buildings and some classics as well: **www.BostonTop10.com**

Just Listed: Find it here first—3 Bed/2 Bath Colonial

Great Neighborhood—Large Yard—Under 500K

www.jonsmithrealtyteam.com/JustListed1

Include videos and photos with your ads when it makes sense, based on the platform. Remember, these are social media platforms, and most of them are very focused on images. Keep your content relevant so people will like, share, comment, and interact.

If you would like more information on specific tools to develop these pages or further example of ads, please visit www.explosivesalesgrowth.com/realestate.

This chapter could be an entire book. In fact, several books have already been written on how to leverage social media in growing a business. We have included several of these titles on our book list for a deeper dive into several of the topics. That list is also available on the website listed above so we can update it and keep the content fresh.

SOCIAL MEDIA SUCCESS RITUALS

Daily:

- Review posts from past clients and sphere of influence and like or comment as appropriate. (Watch for life-altering events such as engagement, marriage, children, divorce, jobs, and relocation.)
- Post content on your social media business pages.
- Private message at least five people.

Weekly:

- Use private messages to request contact information to add to your database.
- Run ads or boost posts for quality content that sends prospects to landing pages for lead generation.

Monthly/Quarterly:

- Post success stories about clients you have helped.

Chapter 8

ONLINE LEADS

We talked about ways to generate online leads through social media and advertising on social media. This chapter focuses on gathering leads through landing pages online. We have two basic ways of doing this. The first and simplest is to pay someone else to generate the lead. This is what you are doing when you pay Zillow, Trulia, Realtor, or any other third-party site for sending you online leads. They generate the lead by people on their website who request more information on a property or pricing information on their own property. The second way is to generate the leads yourself with your own content and your own landing pages.

The Good, The Bad, and The Ugly

The benefit of purchasing the leads from some third-party sites is three-fold:

1. You don't have to create the site or the landing page.
2. You are not responsible for providing the content.

3. Most of the time, the leads actively searched for real estate on a real estate web page.

The downside of these online lead generation programs starts with the fact they compete directly with agents for their own leads since most of the leads are generated from your own listing data that you post on their site. Second, they are costly. When I first purchased leads from Zillow, I could get twenty to thirty leads per month for only a few hundred dollars. A few years later, I would need to spend $1,000-$1,500 per month to get the same number of leads.

Not that these online lead providers are not worthwhile. It is important that you are cognizant of your monthly budget, keeping track of where you are spending your money, and measuring your return on investment. Where most agents fall short is not in where they get their leads but rather in their own follow-up.

We interviewed Lisa Chinatti, top-producing agent whose team closed over 200 units in 2017, about some of their follow-up techniques for online leads. Over 40 percent of her business, approximately 80 units, came from Zillow.

Best Practices for Online Lead Follow-Up

Speed to lead matters. People are clicking buttons online. These days, they expect an immediate response. If they do not get the answer they are looking for in the next couple minutes, they will just click another button and another agent may get the same lead.

One call and one email is not enough. Some agents will make the mistake of only calling or emailing once and when they get no response, they will consider the lead a "bad lead." Instead, you should attempt to contact leads multiple times in the first few days.

Make an attempt every day for the first ten days.

Online leads could be six to eighteen months away from making an actual purchase when they start looking around online. One reason they may not be answering your calls is because they feel like they would waste your time. They are not ready yet. You may try addressing that in one of your contacts by saying that most people start the home-buying process up to eighteen months before they are ready to buy, so they know speaking with a real estate agent early on is normal and even recommended. Schedule regular contact to provide value and build the relationship to support them when they are ready.

Give Them What They Want

When following up with these leads, we need to consider the prospect and what they need. They did not click on a button that said, "Please have an agent call me ten times this week and sell me on why I should work with them as a buyer agent." Typically, all they wanted was to find out more information about a listing. Oftentimes they believed they were reaching out to the listing agent. They may have been looking for an appointment to see the property. Your call should reflect meeting their needs based on their current situation.

When you call, offer the information they were looking for. Use this conversation as an opportunity to ask great questions about what they are looking for in a home by discussing what they liked or disliked about the one they clicked for more information. Your conversation might sound something like the example below.

> **Agent:** "Hi, is this Jennifer?"
>
> **Online Lead:** "Yes. Who's calling?"
>
> **Agent:** "This is (Your Name) with (Your Company). I am calling with the information you were looking for about the home at (Address). Did you have a specific question about the property or were you looking to schedule a showing?"

The call could go in a few different directions. Your job is to engage them about this property and their property search in general. Whether they ask for more information or a showing, let them know you are logging into MLS to pull up the property now, and use that time to ask them some questions, such as:

- What made you inquire about this property?
- What did you like about it?
- Have you looked at any other properties yet?
- What else are you looking for in a home?
- What's prompting the move?

Again, make sure you are providing the information about the property they called about. These questions should all be conversational. It shouldn't sound like an inquisition. Near the end of the conversation, give them a good reason to meet with you in person.

> **Agent:** "I would love to schedule a time to get you in to see this property. Would you be open to looking at a few properties that would meet your needs at the same time for comparison?"

You are looking for an opportunity to sit with the client for a buyer consultation before just running around showing properties. There is no need to waste your time or the prospect's time if they are not ready to buy or have not decided what they want yet. Your job is to help narrow down the options based on their needs and wants. That is much easier to do with an actual consult. Remember that they had not likely planned to meet with an agent when they called, so you may get pushback. You need to show them the value in you.

> **Agent:** "I know your time is valuable, and I have learned through experience that by meeting together for thirty minutes to identify what you want in a home, I can save you ten to

> twenty hours of searching for the perfect home. I could meet this afternoon at 4:00 or tomorrow at 11:00 right before looking at this property. When would be the best time for you?"

You will save time for both you and your prospects by narrowing the search to only look at properties that meet their top needs and wants. When there are lots of choices, you can help them be pickier. When there are fewer options, you may use this as a coaching opportunity to widen their options, increase their price point, or lower their expectations to purchase a home. If they feel as though they are not ready to meet with an agent yet, it may not be worth running around showing them homes. Spend time qualifying your leads and then create a follow-up plan based on their needs.

Qualify the Lead

We put undue pressure on both ourselves and our leads when we attempt to set an appointment with every contact. While meeting with people face to face is a great way to establish a relationship, it can also be a waste of time to run around with people who are not ready, willing and able to purchase yet. There may be additional steps we can walk them through first to prepare them to purchase the home of their dreams.

Begin with a phone conversation to discuss their wants and needs and see if those match up with their ability or readiness to purchase. The easiest way is to start by asking if they have met with a lender yet. Have they received a pre-approval letter or a purchase amount they can afford? Did the lender check their credit? Did the lender require income verification like paystubs or a W-2 yet?

For their current living situation, is there anything that needs to happen in order to buy? Are they in a lease that lasts another six months? Do they have a home they need to sell in order to buy?

What do they owe on their current property? What are they planning to put down on the new one? Is their down payment money caught up in their current equity?

Qualifying the leads will help you decide how hot the leads are for follow-up. They will also help you determine how to best help them take the next step toward achieving their goal of home ownership. We could set an appointment to meet with them and one of our lenders. We could help connect them with a credit repair company if needed or we could meet at their home to determine their current value and what they might have for a down payment after selling their property.

Generating Your Own Online Leads

You have the ability to generate online leads through your own website by providing great content. While it may be difficult to compete with the real estate juggernauts when it comes to generating visitors to your site, you have unique opportunities. You are the local expert. You have the ability to provide hyper-local content that will attract local people to your website. You just need to focus on your unique opportunities and exploit them.

I discussed this topic with Lori Ballen, top agent and owner of Rank Like a Boss. Lori coaches agents on how to grow their online presence through content and SEO strategy. For content creation, you need to choose a topic. Take that topic a mile deep and a mile wide. Consider all the different ways you could discuss this topic. Then continually build out quality pieces of content on the topic. Next share the content through different social media avenues. Evergreen content that is relevant for a long time can be dripped out multiple times, knowing it will not be seen by everyone when posted only once.

When you provide great free content, people will register for additional content. If I love your article and you have a free list or guide I can get via email, then I am likely willing to provide you a valid email address. You will use links to offers and landing pages from within your content to collect contact information from site visitors so you can reach out to them and stay in contact. This will allow you to continually send new content to your email list. It will also create an excellent source of online leads at little to no cost other than minimal website hosting fees and the time to write and promote your content.

Your listings will also provide a great source of content. You can use your listings to create blog posts, social media posts, and email content as ways to generate new leads and stay in touch with current leads. There are three main ways to generate your own online leads through your site. The first is organic search results from search engines by having your web content rank based on local real estate topics for which people may be searching. The second is pay-per-click (PPC) advertising in search engines where you pay to be at the top of those search results pages. The third is social media advertising where you pay to land in front of people on social media sites and divert them to your own content through ads.

Organic search is the longest play. It will take a long time to build out all the content to rank at the top of the pages. Use an SEO strategist to find topics that make sense for you to post about to find your way to the top of the right pages. We share tools on the resource page for deciding how to choose your topics based on what you enjoy and what people are searching for in your area. Building these pages once creates an opportunity for a lifetime of lead generation. Unlike listing information, which changes regularly, content about local restaurants, schools, and things to do may generate local real estate leads for a long time. You can promote these pages and posts over and over again on social media. The initial investment of time may be large, but it can pay off as a long-term strategy. If you enjoy creating content and digging into the numbers for traffic, engagement, leads, etc., then this may just be the way for you to build your business.

Pay-per-click advertising provides a great way to put your content in front of people when you have not yet gotten the organic reach you were hoping for. You may find that a certain post is converting well on Facebook, with people on your email list, or with web visitors. That post may be a good candidate for paid ads to generate additional traffic. This will be a way to amplify your results. Sometimes these ads are overlooked, since people will scroll down to the organic results. However, you don't have to pay for those who scroll past your ad. If you have quality content and you only have to pay for people who click to get to your content, it may a be worthwhile way to generate extra traffic to your site.

Social media advertising will allow you to collect contact information before people ever see your content. The landing page is simple and may even allow them to register using their login information from the social media site they are on using such tools as Facebook Login. This ensures you get correct contact information and simplifies the process, allowing the user to more easily register. Remember that you are disrupting people on social media when you place content in front of them. They likely did not come to Facebook, Twitter, LinkedIn, or Instagram looking for a home. Even if you do get them to click on an interesting ad, you have to get them over the hurdle of engaging after they click. These leads could be even further away from being ready to buy or sell real estate. It doesn't make them bad leads; it means they may take longer to convert.

You will need a longer-term plan to reach out to the online leads who are not ready to act right away. While you may only convert a small percentage to immediate clients, I have seen agents convert 10 percent or more of their online leads over the following year or so through ongoing email marketing. Make sure you have a system in place to track how these leads engage with your emails. Who opens? Who clicks the links? Then follow up with those who are engaging and returning to your site.

ONLINE LEADS SUCCESS RITUALS

Daily:

- Respond immediately to all new online leads via all methods possible including calls, texts and emails.
- Follow up with any new online leads from the past ten days.
- Establish search criteria and send listing alerts.
- Find new leads on social media and connect.

Weekly:

- Speak with vendors such as lenders and credit improvement consultants to ensure proper follow-up with leads.
- Send email blasts of new listings and price drops to buyer leads.
- Call any online leads past their first ten days and inside ninety days.
- Send handwritten follow-up notes.

Monthly/Quarterly:

- Choose a day to call all leads from the past six to twelve months who have not yet responded or with whom you lost contact.

Chapter 9

SECONDARY TRANSACTIONS

have based this entire book on the three L's of real estate, taught in depth in Gary Keller's book, *The Millionaire Real Estate Agent*. The three L's are leads, listings, and leverage.

We have focused on leads so far and a few systems to leverage. This chapter focuses on listings although it is less about getting listings and more about how to use the listings you have at a high level to drive more listing and buyer leads.

"Secondary transactions" may be a new term for some, but I think of them as any transaction that I generate from one of my listings.

Imagine if every time you listed a property, your goal was to land two other transactions: a buyer and a seller. Your business would grow exponentially and infinitely. Talk about explosive sales growth. Think about that for a minute. All you have to do is take every listing and turn it into an additional opportunity to convert one buyer and one seller. The one seller would give you an opportunity to do the same thing again, leading to perpetual growth. Not to mention your buyers would become past clients and potential sellers and buyers as repeat business and referral sources.

If there is one chapter I would suggest mastering, it would be this one, because regardless of how you get your initial listing, if you can master this concept you cannot fail.

I know, I get it. Why doesn't everybody learn how to do this if it's so important? Because it's hard. It takes work, and most people are too lazy to put in the work. It also requires systems and a commitment to those systems, which can take time to build and work at a high level. Often, people give up just before they get it figured out. Successful real estate agents are often good at a lot of things, but organizing and systems is not always a natural fit.

Dedicate your time to these practices, and you will see them work. Working secondary transactions often involves ideas from several of the chapters in this book being brought together in one strategy around working your listings. Maybe that makes this powerful strategy one of the most difficult. You have to master several pieces of different strategies or hire someone else to do some of the work.

There is a hidden strength in using this strategy. This super power will show up in your listing consults, making it impossible for a client not to hire you to get their home sold. Why? Because the marketing plan required to implement this strategy at the highest level so closely aligns with the goal of getting your client the most money for their home that the market will allow.

A Multi-Pronged Approach to Marketing

If you have not already, you will run into many agents whose idea of marketing is posting mediocre pictures with lackluster descriptions in MLS and hoping that a buyer agent will sell the home for them.

Not only is this not a great marketing strategy to support getting the home sold fast and for top dollar, but it does little to nothing to generate future business for the listing agent.

This goes back to the old days when agents were the gatekeepers of information. There was no Zillow, Trulia, Realtor or any other of the hundreds or thousands of sites now available online to find listing information. All you had to do was place your listings in MLS and wait for people to walk into the office to find out what homes were for sale in the area. Or they could drive around looking for signs and call the listing agents.

Well, the world has changed. And so has real estate. People can get their information anywhere. Your job is to have them get it from you. This is where you will have the opportunity to meet unrepresented buyers and sellers without paying for someone else to find them for you. It's also a far more effective way to market your listings.

In coaching and training hundreds of real estate agents, I would frequently hear that they were struggling to find people at their open houses who weren't represented by agents already. So I would ask them two questions. The first we will talk about in this chapter, and the second we will discuss in the next chapter on "effective open houses."

Question: How are you getting the word out about your open houses?

Simple question, right? The typical response is a blank stare with a pause for thought before answering through posting in MLS and reaching out to the other agents in the area. (We have reverse prospecting through our MLS in Massachusetts which sends a simple email out to all agents with a matching buyer client search.) Some agents even called the other top local agents to let them know about the open house.

How could anyone expect to meet unrepresented buyers at their listings if the main way that they advertise them is through a tool that only other agents have access to? This is not to say that there are not agents out there taking full advantage of the lead generation opportunity in front of them, but I wouldn't say it is the norm based on my experience.

The best part about this conversation is the opportunity it opens after the realization that they are not going to meet new clients by reaching out to other real estate agents.

The next level is the fact that agents post open houses on third-party sites, and potential homebuyers would often find them online and show up. While this is true, those sites are built for selling the leads to the agent willing to pay the most. For some agents, this is a great way to build a dominant business. And if you aren't the one paying the most, you want to keep traffic off those sites by giving buyers the information in other ways. So far, we have been talking about open houses, but many of these strategies can be used anywhere in the listing process to market the home and generate leads of potential buyers and sellers.

Marketing the Property Benefits Your Seller

Before we go too far down this path, I want to clear up a myth that we are using our listing client's home as a lead generation tool for our own benefit. This is an objection that I hear from agents and clients on occasion, and it's an easy one to handle. Assuming we can agree that the real estate market is like other markets and supply and demand in the current market are what determine the price, then we can move past this idea.

If supply and demand determine the price for which we can sell your home, then the question stands whether the marketing matters if the market is predetermined. (Excuse me for a moment while I geek out with my Economics degree.) We have no control over supply. We cannot stop your neighbors from putting their house on the market. However, the law of supply and demand assumes something. It assumes that information is freely available to everyone. It assumes all potential buyers know that your home is for sale. It assumes that they all find out about the first open house and have an opportunity to write an offer. While your MLS and other agents may have a large percentage of the buyer population covered, there are certainly a large enough percentage of homes that are purchased by someone who was not yet actively looking with an agent. That simple truth can be the difference in getting an offer immediately for asking or above or creating a multiple-offer situation by impacting demand. Changing the demand often changes the value of the property. Just think about how a buyer's mentality changes in a busy spring market after losing out on a home they loved in a multiple-offer situation. Demand shifts based on the thoughts of the buyer. Even in situations with only one offer, the appearance of high demand created by a quality marketing campaign that drives traffic to the home in the first ten days changes the perception of demand. Our job in marketing is to change the perception of demand.

Create Demand for the Property and Find Leads

The activities and strategies used to create demand for your listings will be the same strategies used to increase the number of buyer and seller leads you capture and convert from each of those transactions.

1.) Price the Property Correctly

The first ten times I completed a Comparative Market Analysis (CMA), I had a couple other agents give me what they thought was a fair price for the home. Most of the time, these comps were the comps, and I had it right. In a couple cases, though, the other agent caught something that I missed. It wasn't always drastic. It may have only been 5 percent of the purchase price, but that 5 percent can be a mind-blowing shift in your ability to generate leads and land the highest sale price for your client.

This depends on whether the market is shifting up or down, but one thing remains the same no matter what: the best homes at the best prices always sell the fastest. More people will come look at a good deal. I am not suggesting that you drastically underprice homes with the hope of driving tons of offers way over the asking price and basically auctioning the home. Make sure your client's home is in the best condition and at the best price of every competing home in their immediate price range.

Assuring that you have the right price will drive traffic to the home when you market at a high level like we discuss in this chapter. A high volume of traffic will provide the social proof that there is a high demand for the home. When you walk through an open house and nobody else is there, you don't think, "Man, I need to write an offer now." However, when five other groups walk through at the same time and there are eight cars on the street, then the buyer's attitude about the need to write an offer shifts if they fall in love with the home. The fear of losing out on the house will prompt an emotional decision to write a higher offer.

Traffic also means you, the agent, will talk with more people. Talking with more people about real estate is basically the definition of lead generation. The more real estate conversations we have, the more homes we will sell.

2.) Promote Listings on the Internet

We discussed earlier that people will find your open houses and your listings on third-party property search sites. Our goal is to build an online presence for our listings that highlights them rather than making them one of the many and that creates opportunities to interact with potential buyers. Potential buyers are often potential sellers.

Promotion at this level starts with content that people will stop and look at. There is so much garbage on the Internet that quality content will stand out. This starts with choosing quality photographs and incorporating videos as well as virtual tours. When we create a blog post, a single property website, print materials, or social media posts, the photography and design have a huge impact on the response we will receive. If a picture is worth a thousand words, what do you think thirty quality photos are worth?

If we planned to make all the information free for the taking, then the quality may not matter, but remember that aside from just marketing the property, we are also lead generating. The first step in generating leads is to capture their information. People are bombarded with opt-ins and sign-ins. Your content has to be so valuable that leads would give you their actual email address or phone number in order to get more of that content. There is a value exchange. If you find that you are not generating the number of leads you want from your content, then maybe the content needs to be better. It needs to give enough value for free that people would "pay" for more with their contact information.

That being said, you must give just enough content to attract attention and then link to a landing page for people to continue getting more content. Facebook ads and boosted posts should offer quality photos and enough information to pique someone's interest before linking to a landing page where they will offer their name, email address, and even their phone number to see the rest of the pictures, get a video walk-through, or find out the price and location. Whatever you are offering, it has to provide something that they cannot get for free anywhere else.

3.) Promote Your Listings to Your Database

You have spent valuable time and money developing a database of people who could be potential buyers for your listings. They could also be potential sellers who have no desire to purchase your listing but now want to list with you based on the impression you made by promoting all of your listings so well. The email should be simple and drive people back to your website. Most tools at this point will show you who has opened those emails and who has clicked to return to your site. This is your list of prospects you should be following up with more frequently. People who consistently click your emails and go back to your site are raising their hands as someone you could help resolve a real estate need.

4.) Create a Physical Presence in the Market

The Internet is a powerful tool. You can reach your clients inexpensively on a regular basis with little time and energy. However, this will never replace the relationships built with face-to-face conversations. In order to be effective in turning listings into additional listing and buyer clients, you need to get your name out there and have conversations with people to build relationships.

Start by making sure people know you are the agent. The listing provides an opportunity for signage. While you have to follow the rules of the city, town, or development, make sure you take advantage of every opportunity to have properly placed signs. With the right directional signs and open house signs around the neighborhood, one listing can make it appear like you have listings all over town.

Whether you knock on doors or call around the neighborhood is a matter of preference and other circumstances like distance between homes or weather conditions. In many cases, agents are afraid to reach out to neighborhoods. People don't typically like cold calling.

What I want people to realize about promoting your listings, though, is that it can be a super warm approach. Try this script:

> "Hey there. I'm (Agent Name) with (Agent Company), and I am not sure if you saw the sign yet, but we just listed (Address) down the street. I wanted to let people in the neighborhood know we are having our first open house this weekend, so if you see a bunch of extra cars in the neighborhood, that is probably why. We are doing a bunch of marketing and expect a large turnout for a home in such a great neighborhood."
>
> "Also, we are opening a half hour early for neighbors. Now, I know you probably will not move down the street, but we know a lot of neighbors like to have a comparison for what their house might be worth or they may know someone else interested in moving to the area. We would love for you to stop by if you are around. It might be a chance for you to pick your neighbor. Do you know of anyone who might want to move to the neighborhood?"
>
> {If they say no:} "No worries. Could you do one thing for me though? Like I said, we expect a ton of traffic through the open house, and since it is such a nice neighborhood, we will get some buyers who love the neighborhood but this particular house isn't the right fit for them. Will you just let me know if you talk to anyone else who is thinking about selling in the neighborhood? I may be able to connect them with some awesome buyers. Thanks so much for your time. Hopefully we will see you this weekend."

The thing I love about this script is that it puts no pressure on them. It's sort of like a public service announcement, just letting them know there may be a bunch of people in the area. And it gives them an invitation to the open house, along with two opportunities to offer a referral or say they are thinking about moving.

You can increase the effectiveness by having door hangers printed with open house information on the front and a very similar message on the back. Take these with you when going door-to-door and leave one at each home where no one answers.

We will talk more about what to do in the actual open houses to convert some of this traffic into clients in the next chapter.

5.) Look Like the Five-Star Option

We talked earlier about the importance of quality images and print materials. If someone were to walk into your listing or next open house, what would your materials tell them about you as an agent? Are you throwing black-and-white MLS printouts on the table or countertop? Do you have colored brochures? Is there neighborhood information?

Here's the deal: if I am a buyer and I go out to look at open houses, I am not only checking out one house. That means I get to compare the homes I see on the same day. If I also need to sell my current home or haven't picked an agent to work with yet on the buy side, then I am also comparing the agents I meet. The one who stands out as having market knowledge - looking professional, helpful, and trustworthy - and providing useful information is the one who will land the client. Are you using these listings as an opportunity to apply for the position of agent for everyone you come into contact with? Some of them will have agents. For the ones who don't, are you willing to risk not landing them as clients? What's the cost of that missed opportunity?

It's important to remember that converting listings into additional listing and buyer clients requires a combination of all of these things. While getting good at any one or two will help your business, it's the combination that will create explosive growth. When you hear people say that they see your name everywhere, then that's when you know you are doing it right. We need to become the first person they think of when they think about real estate.

SECONDARY TRANSACTION SUCCESS RITUALS

Daily:

- Call, text, and email all new leads generated from listings.
- Respond to all comments on social media posts and ads.
- Invite anyone who liked your social media posts to like your business page.

Weekly:

- Door-knock a neighborhood of fifty homes for your new listings, open houses, or just solds.
- Circle call a neighborhood for invites to open houses.
- Email blast your new listings to your database.
- Send direct mail to alert a neighborhood to your listing.
- Target social media ads to neighborhoods where you have new listings.
- Run open houses in your listings.
- Place signs around your listings with directional signage.

Monthly/Quarterly:

- Send an email blast of a new blog post to all past leads from your previous listings.

Chapter 10

EFFECTIVE OPEN HOUSES

How many times have you pulled up to meet your client at an open house and watched the agent who was hosting the open house running to tie up the balloon, unlock the door, and turn on all the lights three minutes after the scheduled start time?

An open house is not a party where we show up fashionably late to appear busy. An open house is an event. More specifically, it is a lead generation event. Whether it's your listing does not matter. This is an opportunity to display yourself as a market expert to potential buyers and sellers. If you give up your weekends to work open houses, I want you to make sure they are successful in not just promoting your listings but also in growing your business.

Choose the Right Open Houses

If you have your own listings to hold open, then you have less control over this, but you have some control because you priced the house accordingly, and you have advertised according to our promotion plan. If you are covering the open house for another agent in your office, then you want to do a few things to guarantee you have the best chance of generating a lead.

When choosing open houses, you need to set yourself up for success. I would make sure to only run open houses for agents who will let you promote the listing on your site. It will still show them as the listing agent, but you should be able to use the open house to drive buyer leads to landing pages with social media posts and Facebook ads. I would also make sure they are okay with you putting up directional signs with your name and phone number around the area. Reason being that if people get lost trying to find the home, it won't do them much good to call the listing agent when you are the one covering the open house. Also, I wouldn't drive around putting signs up to promote the listing agent. So the first thing is to only cover for agents who want you to drive traffic to their listings. Why wouldn't they? I am guessing they want the house to sell.

Second, choose homes that have something new about them. You want to find a home that is either new to the market, has recently been staged or had work done, has new photos, has a recent price adjustment or anything else that would make people come out and look at it. A home that has been on the market for sixty days with the same price and photos is not likely to be a winning open house for lead generation.

Third, choose homes in the area where you want to sell homes. If farming is one of your methods to generate business, then I would look for every opportunity to work open houses that are within your farm. Remember, we are looking for people to say, "I see you everywhere."

The last tip is to choose homes in a price range where there are likely to be a lot of buyers. I know there is this desire to sell homes where the price is higher so you can sell fewer homes and still make

more money. I get it. And you should work toward growing your average sale price when possible. However, for open houses, I would prefer to have a home right around the average or median sale price for the location. Promoting homes in that price range will drive more traffic than the handful of homes in the area that are double the price. Statistically, I have a better chance of meeting an unrepresented buyer or seller if I can generate more traffic through the open house.

Tell Everybody About the Open House

Remember that the open house is a lead generation event. The more conversations you have about real estate, the more homes you will sell. Use this opportunity to tell everyone that you are an active real estate professional. Most people will have no idea if you are the listing agent when you promote your open houses.

Take advantage of directional signs that contain your contact information and even consider hanging balloons on the signs to make them stand out. Post on social media the time and location of your open house, along with a few photos of the home, and invite people who live locally to stop by and visit even if they aren't going to purchase the property. Remember that your sphere of influence already knows, likes, and trusts you, and we want them to think of you every time they think of real estate. Aside from just posting on social media, you can also run advertising to reach more people. If you are spending money on ads, then I would drive people to some sort of landing page where you can collect their contact information to reach out to them in the future.

Don't forget to call around the neighborhood or knock on doors to invite people to the open house. Face-to-face interactions will foster relationship building. The simple script we shared in the last chapter will allow you to invite people to the open house while talking up your marketing efforts and inviting them to refer buyers and sellers. It's a soft script with little ask but which will inform the neighborhood and lead to additional traffic and leads.

Look and Sound Like a Pro

Try to incorporate all the senses into the experience of the open house. One strength of open houses is that people have the ability to *see* what the home looks like in person, *touch* the walls and countertops, *hear* the sounds in the neighborhood, *feel* the warmth, and *smell* the fragrances of the home. Look to control each of these senses as best you can to put the best foot forward in the home. Ian Lobas, who runs a $25 million team, says they cook cinnamon rolls at 200° before an open house so that the scent will permeate the home for hours.

Your appearance and that of the home will impact the first impressions people have of you as an agent when they walk in the door. Leave yourself ample time to walk through the home, turn on all the lights, open curtains and shades as needed, tidy up, and be prepared when people walk through the door. Don't be the agent rushing around and fumbling through keys or the lockbox when people arrive. Also, dress for success. My favorite rule for dress is to always dress one step above where you expect most of your clients to be dressed. If they would be in polo shirts, you wear a shirt and tie. If you expect to see jeans and t-shirts, then maybe a polo shirt is fine. You will have to ultimately decide what your personal brand will be, but you want people to feel comfortable with you and respect you as a professional.

Aside from how you look, what you have to say is likely even more important. Make sure you know the basics about the home even if it is not your listing. If you don't know the right answer, it is fine to say that you will find out from the sellers, but if they ask about something already on the MLS sheet then you should know the answers. Remember you provide value by knowing the market, which means you should know about the home you are standing in.

Where you have the ability to stand out in the crowd is in how you handle the conversations with people who attend the open house. If you are knowledgeable about the market and ask the right questions, you may write an offer on the property or help the buyers find a home that is a better fit for them.

For example, if you are showing a property in a certain price range that, with three bedrooms, is a little on the smaller side, then you should prepare information on slightly larger homes that possibly have four bedrooms in the same price range. If the home you are holding open has a tiny yard, be prepared to talk about a property with a larger backyard.

If you study the property, along with other local properties with different amenities and price points, and you ask the right questions, you have the ability to build a relationship with a potential client and show value from the first conversation. If you have been struggling to convert open house leads in the past, it is likely that you were waiting until your follow-up on Monday morning to start the process. The following questions are the ones I like to ask during an open house to get people to open up and then set an appointment later.

Note: Make sure you follow the agency laws in your state and ask your broker to clarify which conversations you can have in the property. The laws vary in different states.

Open House Script

As people are finishing up walking through the home, run through the following script.

> **Agent:** "I would love to offer some feedback to the sellers. Could you tell me what you liked best about the home?"

Buyers: "We like the layout and the size. We really like the kitchen."

Agent: "If you could change one thing about the house, what would it be?"

Buyers: "The busy street. It is a lot busier than we expected."

Agent: "Anything else?"

Buyers: "We would like a flat backyard as well. We want to be able to entertain outdoors."

Agent: "Have you guys happened to see 123 XYZ Street yet? It has a lot of the same features, only it's in a quiet little neighborhood and has a nice patio and yard."

Buyers: "No, we haven't seen it yet."

Agent: (Take out your favorite app and show them a few pictures.) "I am here until 1:00, but I can see if I can get you guys in there later today or tomorrow."

Buyers: "Tomorrow would be great."

Agent: "Great. What's the best number to reach you once I get the appointment set?"

Buyers: "555-555-5555"

Agent: "Perfect. And what email can I send a copy of the listing information to?"

Buyers: "abcdefg@gmail.com"

Agent: "Sounds good. I look forward to seeing you guys tomorrow. I will call you later to confirm the time."

Here's the thing. If the people like this house that we are standing in, then I am going help them write an offer and get this home sold. However, we know that only one person will buy this home and lots of other people who attend the open house will not buy this particular home for one reason or another. If I can offer those people value, like finding them a home that fits their needs during our conversation, then they are far more likely to choose me as their agent.

What people care most about is what they want. As much as I want to get feedback for the sellers and the listing agent if it isn't me, I am even more concerned about what the people standing in front of me need and want. I know that if they tell me what they like and dislike about this home, I can turn that conversation into a brief consultation about what is important to them about their next home. All I have to do is determine what they want and show them how I can help them get it. It is hard to say "no" to your own goals.

Ask Great Questions

Where most salespeople falter is when they try to always provide the answers. While knowledge is important, the conversation is controlled by the person asking the questions. Asking the right questions at the right time will help people to open up in conversation and share with you what they need to move forward.

This is the unscripted part of the script. The scripted questions you ask will be similar every time. However, your ability to listen to the person in front of you and interact with what they are saying will allow you to develop a relationship quickly. Interacting not reacting is what will allow you to build a trusting relationship. When you think you are done asking questions, ask one more.

When I ask, "What do you love about the house," I know the next question in the script is, "If you could change one thing about the house, what would it be?" That question is not the very next thing out of my mouth, however. Often, there is a follow-up question based on their response. If they say, "We really love the open concept," my response might be, "What do you love about the open concept? Why is it important to you?"

There are several ways this conversation can move and flow. Here is the thing: you cannot care so much about the outcome that you don't spend the time to get to know the people. I want them to tell me they really want to be able to host their whole family for holidays. I want to know their family parties have twenty to thirty people at them. I want to know if they can picture them all fitting here. I want to know where they think everyone would congregate.

I want these potential clients 100 percent in or out on whatever home they purchase. I want them to know I am just as happy if they are 100 percent out. It's not my job to push them to buy a home that doesn't meet their needs. It is my job to understand what they want so well that I know which home they are going to buy before they even walk in the door. In fact, that is one of the best feelings as an agent. When you can honestly say to your client that you knew this would be the one, it means you were listening intently. It means you knew what was really important to the client. It means you asked the right questions. And if you can provide that level of caring for every person who walks through your open house whether they have an agent or not, it will change your business. You will attract people to you instead of having to chase them. People want to interact with people who want to help them get what they want.

OPEN HOUSE SUCCESS RITUALS

Daily:

- Reach out to agents to see who needs coverage for the best open houses.

Weekly:

- Build single-property pages and landing pages for open houses to lead capture online.

- Post directional signs around the neighborhood where you will host an open house.

- Review similar homes to discuss with potential clients at the open house in case the home being held open is not a fit.

- Call or door-knock around the neighborhood to invite neighbors.

- Place door hangers with open house information on doors when people are not home during door-knocking.

- Call your sphere of influence and invite them to visit you at the open house when you are in their neighborhood.

Monthly/Quarterly:

- Send an email blast of similar listings to all past open house leads.

Chapter 11

JUST LISTED/JUST SOLD

We discussed using information on just listed and just sold homes in chapter 9 when we discussed marketing ideas for creating secondary transactions. Remember that a secondary transaction arrives any time we can convert a listing into an additional listing or buying client. One concept in that chapter is to promote each phase of the selling process, including properties that are coming soon, just listed, under contract, sale pending, and just sold. These phases create opportunities to let the world—especially the hyper-local world of that particular neighborhood—know that you are the real estate expert in the area.

These opportunities present themselves any time a home comes on the market or closes. The listings do not have to be your own in order to build a conversation around them. The majority of agents in your area will not call around the neighborhood or knock on doors and let everyone know about their new listing or their listing that just sold. Most of them will not even mail out a postcard.

I am just going to come out and say it. Many of the agents you are competing with are not really competing. Most agents are simply taking the business that falls in their lap. This provides an incredible advantage for an agent who is willing to go out and find business. Prospecting these neighborhoods is not expensive or difficult, and you can do it whether you are a brand-new agent or someone who has a lifetime of experience in the field.

Two of the simplest real estate events in the world to promote are new listings and properties that just sold. The reason they are so simple is that you can look up everything in MLS based on how recently it came on the market. You could find a listing that just came on yesterday or today in one of the neighborhoods you prefer to work in and let everyone know its availability and the listing price. Make sure you in no way make it sound as though a listing is yours when it is not. Integrity is an integral part of running a business based on trusting relationships. There will be a giant sign in the yard letting people know who the listing agent is, if there is not one already. You are simply informing people about what is happening in their local market. This new listing is about to become a comparable sale (comp) for their property and therefore valuable information to know.

The Value You Bring to the Neighborhood

We talk about this in almost every chapter. You must add value to the prospect before they ever become your client. They could go look up this new listing information online pretty much anywhere once they see the sign go up. What you bring to the table is your own set of thoughts, insights, and opinions, based on research and experience, about what may happen with this property and, more importantly, how what happens with this property may affect the value of their property.

People care about the value of their property for many reasons whether they are planning to sell immediately or not. For many people, their home is their most valuable asset. If they do not have large investments, their home could be the only appreciating asset they own. The way it appreciates and where it stands should be of significance to the owner. Your ability to discuss how these facts impact them is what creates your value proposition in building a relationship with these potential clients.

The Just Listed Script

You can use the following script whether you knock on doors or call around the neighborhood.

> **Agent:** "Hey, I am (Your Name) with (Brokerage Name), and I am just reaching out to let you know about a new property that just came on the market that may impact the value of your home."
>
> **Homeowner:** "Okay."
>
> **Agent:** "This may seem like a strange call, but I know most homeowners are interested in the value of their home because of what a big investment it is, so we wanted to let you know that the home at (Listing Address) just went on the market yesterday, and it's listed for $600,000. What do you think about that price?"
>
> **Homeowner:** "It seems (high, low, about right)." Or: "I am not sure about that house. I don't know how big it is or anything about the condition."
>
> **Agent:** "Here's why I wanted to reach out. I don't know if you have ever thought about selling your home, but when we price homes we base them on other homes that have recently sold nearby. What buyers are willing to pay in your neighborhood determines the value; does that make sense?"

> **Homeowner:** "Yes."
>
> **Agent:** "So if you were thinking about selling or even refinancing in the next six months, this property could be one of the comparable sales, or comps, used to determine the value of your home. Have you considered taking advantage of the current market and selling your home?"

The Response

There are three answers that the homeowner may give at this point. I guess there are actually four, but I will leave out the option where they might swear at or hang up on you as there is little to do other than courteously thank them for their time and let them off the phone (or move on if they've already hung up). The next three possible answers are "no," "yes," and anything in between.

The "no" response may or may not be followed by an explanation, such as:

- We just bought the house last year.
- We plan on staying here until we die.
- We have no reason to move. I don't care what this house is worth, I wouldn't sell it for $10 million.

These are the ones I would consider a definitive "no." What's great about these is that we can cross them off the list for now and focus on those considering a move. Remember no matter what people say, situations change, and many people buy and sell homes for unexpected reasons, so nobody is a "no" forever in my book. However, I do not want to waste time or bother people who are not potential clients unless they want me to stay in touch.

The "yes" response is the unicorn that makes rainbow ice cream. This is the one we are dreaming about. This could turn into a listing appointment either on the spot or scheduled for the next day or two. As soon as I hear that "yes," I start my consultation as if we were planning to sign the listing agreement that day. That means a full-on needs analysis to find out why they are thinking about selling and, more importantly, where are they going to live when we sell their home? What is their ideal living situation that would make them want to sell tomorrow? Again, asking powerful questions here and letting them know that you are there to help them get what they want is what will land you this prospect as a client.

There are two benefits to finding your client through this style of prospecting. The first is that the majority of sellers will still only meet with one agent, and you are likely speaking with them first because you went to them. You did not wait for them to look for an agent. The second benefit is that by coming to them, you showed them your tenacity and willingness to go out and get the job done. I am willing to bet that not a ton of agents were calling or knocking on their door. This isn't a For Sale By Owner or expired listing we are talking about. You also started the conversation by showing them your knowledge of the market and how you stay on top of what is coming on the market and closing. This helps you show your value as the market expert.

Just Sold Homes

Homes that just sold are now comparable sales in the neighborhood that do affect their value. Sold data is typically much harder for homeowners to access unless they check the newspaper or public records on a regular basis. The conversation is not drastically different from that of the just listed script other than now you are talking about the actual sale price of the property, which will provide better data for their home valuation.

This also makes for a great follow-up conversation for anyone you interacted with in the neighborhood when the property was listed. You now have the ability to continue building the relationship by showing how you follow up and by explaining how the pricing strategy worked. How long was the house on the market? Did they get more or less than asking? Did they see any of the marketing done by the agent?

The Tools

To work just listed and just sold properties, you will need some tools. Depending on your location, the MLS system you use, and your access to public records, much of the resources you need may already be found in the tools you have. If you will knock on doors, make sure to follow the local rules and laws. This will require little in the way of technology, though, as you can just go to maps.google. com and choose the streets you plan to canvass. If you will send direct mail, you will have the option of bulk mail or Every Door Direct Mail® (EDDM) through the USPS. If the neighborhood overlaps well with a mail route, EDDM will be the cheaper and easier option.

If you call around neighborhoods, then it will be worth paying for a directory of phone numbers you can access by neighborhood. Many of these systems also come with email addresses, cell phone numbers, and landline numbers. Several also have dialer options to speed the number of calls you can make, and some even pair them with FSBO and expired listing leads. We cover a bunch of these on the website if you would like more information. (The link again is www.explosivesalesgrowth.com/realestate.)

Combining mail with knocking on doors and calling around the neighborhood will return the greatest results as your frequency will gain you trust with the neighborhood, as long as you are providing value. Regardless of your method, remember that the strategy is based on providing homeowners with useful information that impacts their home valuation as a way to start a conversation about real estate. As with every lead generation source, the more conversations you have about real estate, the more homes you will sell.

JUST LISTED/JUST SOLD SUCCESS RITUALS

Daily:

- Search MLS for newly listed and newly sold properties in your area.
- Practice your scripts for calls and door-knocking.
- Call fifty homes around a new listing or newly sold property.

Weekly:

- Door-knock fifty doors around a recently listed or sold property.
- Send postcards for your own just listed and just sold properties.

Monthly/Quarterly:

- Send a market update with newly sold data and new listing data to the neighborhood.

Chapter 12

FARMING

n this context, farming is not raising livestock and growing veg-
etables. Farming in real estate involves choosing a specific group
of people with whom you would like to conduct business and
consistently marketing to them over a long period to develop market
share. Farming could be demographic, based on specific qualities, or
geographic – based on certain locations or neighborhoods.

There has been a long-standing lore and legend of the direct mail
trial in real estate. I have heard it told in several trainings and have
even repeated the story myself. Whether there was an actual study or
it's just a story doesn't matter since it illustrates key points required
for effectively farming.

The story goes like this: To test the theory of creating top-of-mind
awareness, a study was completed. After choosing a farm area, the
researchers surveyed the neighborhood to ask who was the number
one real estate agent in the neighborhood. Some people didn't have an
answer. Some named an agent they knew of, but there was no certain
agent that held any significant mind share within the farm area.

For the next two months, they mailed the farm each week with the same fictitious agent's information. At the end of the two months, they surveyed the neighborhood again, and this time you can guess the top agent in the neighborhood.

You got it: the large majority chose the fictitious agent more than any other agent. And just eight or nine pieces of mail later. Whether the story is true, we can pull several best practices from the parable. The first thing I would look at is the fact that they chose a neighborhood in which no agent had secured substantial market share. They mailed consistently to the same group of people over time. Consistent messaging created mind share.

Where the story falls short is that it doesn't create any business. Creating mind share is only the first step in lead generating from a farm. Two months is also far too short a period. Often, agents would give up after spending two months' worth of time, effort, and energy on a farm if they did not get a listing. Just because people in the neighborhood recognize you as the agent of choice through your mail campaign does not mean that those same people are even thinking about selling right now. The money in farming comes from the longevity and consistency.

Committing to the Strategy

If you are thinking about sending a single piece of mail, or even a half dozen per year to a farm, I would try to talk you into better spending your money elsewhere. As we talked about earlier in this book, a common mistake of most agents is that they dabble in different strategies but do not commit to one or two strategies that they will implement at the highest level.

This strategy of farming only provides results and return on investment as a long-term strategy, so if you are not committed, it will likely just cost you money. If you remain committed and slowly grow your farm over time, you should see results that will serve the expansion of your farm area.

Consistency is Key

A few paragraphs ago, we talked about generating mind share. Essentially, you are working to become the first agent people think of when they think about real estate in your farm area. This is important because most sellers continue to work with the first agent that they meet with about selling their house. I suppose part of that comes down to the confidence of the agent they meet with, but a good agent is going to sign the listing at the appointment so there would be no opportunity to meet with anyone else. For those who do meet with two or potentially three agents, who would you guess is most likely to end up landing the listing? Most times, it will be the neighborhood expert.

The idea behind becoming top of mind and gaining mind share is based in the way our brains work. We put things into categories. We then retain the top one, two, or three brands in each of those categories. So when I tell people to think of a brand of sneaker or potato chip, they will typically blurt out the first one that comes to them. When I ask for another, the most common response is an audible pause followed by an "ah?" or "hmm?" When I ask for a third, the pause gets longer. Certain categories do not even allow for a third or fourth response.

So in the category of real estate agents, which one do you want to be?

Exactly. We want to be the first answer people blurt out when they are asked to think of a real estate agent. At a minimum, we want to be the second answer that readily comes out immediately following the first.

So we should consider how brands get to be these category leaders. Think about the marketing budgets of companies like Lays and Nike, two common responses when asked for a potato chip or sneaker brand, respectively. These companies created consistent marketing messages and campaigns through television ads in order to constantly get in front of their target market. They didn't just run one ad and hope to sell a few sneakers or bags of chips. They committed to a message and a strategy. Once they built top of mind, they gained shelf space in retail outlets based on demand and volume, so that their brands are top of mind with consumers based on prime real estate space in the retail outlets at the point of sale.

Everything Points to Consistent and Frequent Touches

For mailing to your farm area, it is important that the message grabs attention, adds value, creates consistent branding, and has a call-to-action. But nothing is as important as the consistency and frequency that your messaging reaches your audience.

Building top-of-mind awareness will take being in front of your farm area regularly. Definitely monthly, but likely a minimum of twice per month, will create results in the right farm area. You may even want to start with more than two pieces per month in a new farm so people get to know who you are quickly. That may speed the process in getting a response.

Notice we did not say to send twelve or twenty-four pieces in a year. Sending six one month and then none for three months will not have the same impact as mailing consistently. Selling a home often happens because of a life event: a job change, a new child, kids graduating and moving out. You need your message in front of the prospect when the time comes for hiring an agent. The unfortunate part is that we have no way of knowing when that will be, so we need to be in front of them all the time.

Choose the Right Farm

Mailing twice a month can become quite an investment when you commit for a long period, so we want to make sure you are generating the return on investment required to keep growing. The easiest way is to make sure of two things. The first is to ensure that there is enough turnover of homes in the neighborhood. We are looking for 6 percent or higher of homes sold in the neighborhood each year. You can figure this out by pulling the number of sold properties for the neighborhood in MLS and then dividing by the number of total houses in the neighborhood. A list of streets will likely be the easiest way to check. You can also do this in a public record search if you can pull the list of streets and sort by last sale date. It may even be worth going back a few years to get a feel for a normal year in that farm area.

The second component is the average sale price or, more importantly, the average commission you would expect to earn from each home you sell in the farm. If you can expect 3 percent per sale and the average sale price is $100,000, then you know you would earn $3,000 for each home. Whereas if you are earning 3 percent on a $400,000 average sale, you can expect a $12,000 average commission. Clearly you need to sell more homes to reach your return on investment goals with lower commissions and average sale prices.

Once you can check off both boxes, then you are on track for choosing the right farm. The last thing to consider is whether another agent already has market share in that farm area. Typically, this will not be an issue. Beware of limiting beliefs in this area. I have heard many agents say that the top agent Cindy So-and-So already sells all the houses in that neighborhood or town. However, if you pull market share numbers as a percentage of homes sold, often that top agent — even though they sell a bunch of homes compared to other agents in the area — still only has single-digit market share numbers of 5 to 8 percent. You may choose a different neighborhood if someone already has the market cornered but be sure that you check your facts by researching the sold homes on MLS to see who is selling them.

Choose the Right Size for Your Farm

Farming is a numbers game. You are hoping to be in front of as many potential sellers as possible, knowing that only a small percentage of them will sell each year. The more people you can reach within your farm, the better your chances will be of seeing some immediate return. At the same time, this can be a significant investment to carry and a costly one if you have to stop after sending five or ten mailers because you have blown your budget by making your farm area too big.

This decision depends on where you are in your business and your finances. Remember, this is an investment, and a long-term investment at that. There are faster and cheaper ways to generate business. Mailing to a farm requires a large investment of money, but it will allow you to expand your business while leveraging your financial investment to free up your time. Also, much of the farming work will be leveraged to other people, so you can invest almost no time in the mailings once you have your systems and leverage in place.

Let's look at a few examples of what different-size farms would cost to reach. We will examine farms of 500; 5,000 and 20,000 to look at costs and expected returns.

Example one:

Say we choose a farm of 500 households, and we intend to mail to them twice a month. That's twenty-four pieces per house per year.

500 x 24 =12,000 pieces

Assuming an average cost per piece of $0.29 to print and another $0.20 to mail, we are looking at $0.49 per piece.

Mailing to this farm for the year will be an investment of $5,880.

Example two:

Now, let's say we choose a farm of 5,000 households, and we intend to mail to them twice a month. That's still twenty-four pieces per house per year, but the total number is much higher.

5,000 x 24 =120,000 pieces

Printing and mailing will become cheaper with our larger farms based on bulk, especially if we are able to use Every Door Direct Mail® (EDDM) to reach an entire section of a city or town. EDDM allows up to 5,000 pieces per mailing. Assuming an average cost per piece of $0.10 to print and another $0.20 to mail, we are looking at $0.30 per piece.

Mailing to this farm for the year will be an investment of $36,000.

Example three:

Now, let's say we choose a farm of 20,000 households, and we again intend to mail to them twice a month. That's twenty-four pieces per house per year.

20,000 x 24 =480,000 pieces

Printing should continue to become cheaper as you increase your bulk order. EDDM allows up to 5,000 pieces per mailing, so we will need four mailing drops. Assuming an average cost per piece of $0.10 to print and another $0.20 to mail, we are looking at $0.30 per piece.

Mailing to this farm for the year will be an investment of $144,000.

These examples are not meant to scare you but rather to help you understand the investment involved in mailing to a farm. I want you to avoid the most common mistake of taking on too much too fast. Agents tend to build farms of 1,000 or 2,000 when they only have the budget for 500. Then they mail regularly for three months or six months. After that, they will often drop from two pieces per month to one or from one per month to once every other month, and then they will stop when they do not see the results they had hoped for and decide that farming doesn't work. Here's the thing. These strategies work when you follow a plan or model and commit to it. They take time. Increase your chances of success by choosing the right size farm, so you can follow through and remain committed to the process.

Once you generate results from your farming efforts, then you can reinvest some of that revenue to grow your farm size. When we interviewed top-producing agent Lisa Chinatti, who closed over 200 units last year with her team, she explained how she had the money to invest so she started with 2,500 homes and now mails to 30,000 homes each month. That is over 60,000 pieces of mail. She built to that volume over the past two years based on the number of listings they took from farming using EDDM. (Check out the interview on the resource page at www.explosivesalesgrowth.com/realestate.)

What is My Expected Return on Investment?

The numbers in every location will be different based on the variables we talked about earlier, like average sale price and commission.

It will also depend on the strength of your marketing plan and the quality of your listing presentation. If you have only ever sold homes for people you knew or were referred to, there was an element of trust when you walked into the home. Establishing that trust quickly will be important with people who have only seen your postcards.

Having completed several trainings on the topic, coached several agents through farming, and interviewed several top agents in writing this book, I have found that the numbers vary wildly. A large problem with the data is that most agents do not track their numbers as well as they should. The best reports that I have seen hover somewhere between 1:100 and 1:150 homes per year, meaning that 1 in every 100 or 150 households that received a mailer completed a transaction with the agent. And these agents are only seeing this conversion after eighteen to twenty-four months of sending mail.

Let's use the 5,000-home farm as an example to measure return based on these numbers. If we use the conversion of 1:150, then we would expect to find thirty-three listings from our farming efforts. If we close 75 percent of those, then we would have closed twenty-five units from this farm. Now the return comes back to average commission. The cost of printing and mailing doesn't change much based on location, so the higher the average commission, the higher the return on investment.

Assuming the average sale price in the United States, $248,000 as of November 2017, and a 3 percent commission, then we would expect $7,440 per closing. Closing twenty-five units with an average commission of $7,440 brings $186,000 in gross commission income (GCI). If you look back at example two, we budgeted for a $36,000 investment to reach 5,000 homes twenty-four times in the year. That would return 5.1 times your investment. Remember, you may not see these numbers in the first or second year.

Improving either the average commission or the conversion ratio would improve the expected return. The average commission comes down to picking the right farm based on average sale prices, which does not necessarily mean highest sale price, and improving your value as a listing agent in order to command higher commissions. Let's look at the ways to increase the conversion ratio, because that may be easier than trying to impact average commissions.

Farms are Not Built by Mail Alone

Mailing twice per month to your farm is a great start to generating a ton of business over time. It is a highly leveraged way to expand, and it can be duplicated in multiple farms. While the return numbers are decent, when you make a long-term commitment to mailing, there are several ways to improve the results. When talking with top agents who use farming as a strategy, a common theme is that people who call them say, "I see you everywhere."

What they mean is, "I see you frequently and everywhere." If you show up in their mailbox twice every month that is a great start. When you cover open houses in your farm area every weekend and posting your directional signs, you are increasing the frequency of your message. When you list a home and post a sign in your farm, you are increasing frequency. When you target a Facebook ad to your farm area, you increase your frequency. When you promote charity events and community events in your mailers and get out and meet the members of your farm, you build relationships. While this requires a larger investment of time and maybe a little money, it builds off the momentum you create from farming and will improve the numbers for the return on investment in that area.

Look for ways to be involved in the neighborhood associations or local sports teams. Sponsor local community events. Compared to what you are spending on mail, you may find these to be small investments that will impact your numbers dramatically. Not only will your numbers increase, but with each listing you increase and upgrade your sphere of influence and create new opportunities to generate secondary transactions and referral business.

FARMING SUCCESS RITUALS

Daily:

- Search MLS for newly listed and newly sold properties in your farm.
- Respond immediately to any new farm leads.

Weekly:

- Hold an open house in your farm.
- Run an ad in social media targeting your farm.
- Visit all new open houses in your farm. Get to know the inside of every home.
- Visit any yard sales or garage sales in your farm.

Monthly/Quarterly:

- Send one or two pieces of direct mail to your farm.
- Hold an event or fundraiser in your farm area.
- Door-knock in your farm to let people know about your event.

Chapter 13

FOR SALE BY OWNER (FSBO)

Each lead generation strategy has its own unique set of advantages and challenges. Most lead generation strategies require us as agents to do the work of finding out who wants to sell their home right now or in the near future. The advantage of working properties listed as For Sale By Owner is that we know one important fact: they want to sell their home now. In fact, they usually have a sign in their yard and some advertisements online, letting us know they are interested in selling their home. Imagine if you could just walk through town and have people raise their hand in the air, yelling, "I want to sell my home." How much easier would that make your job? For Sale By Owner prospects are doing just that.

The challenge to working with For Sale By Owners is often two-fold. The first is that they know real estate agents exist, and yet they chose to list their home for sale without you. They likely had a reason. The most common reason is that they want to save money. For

Sale By Owners believe that listing without an agent will net them more money in their pocket at the end of the transaction. They may have had a bad experience in the past with an agent, but in many cases it simply comes down to money. It's your job as an agent to overcome this objection, and we will talk about how to do just that in a moment.

The second challenge is that you are likely not the only agent trying to win the business from this potential listing client. Some agents may be less-than-tactful in their approach. That often has the opposite effect and can build defensive walls around the client, making them attempt to avoid all agent contact in an effort to stop the calls and mail. There are two things required to overcome this obstacle: a softer approach and some differentiation in your service. Earlier we discussed how most people do not care about price; they care about value. In most cases, these prospects do not believe in or understand the value of a strong agent on their side. That is one of the main reasons they chose to list the property on their own. You need to show them your value. What makes you different? What brings extreme value to your clients?

The Softer Approach

Banging on the door and shoving a listing contract in someone's face is not likely going to get the job done with a For Sale By Owner. We need to take a little time to build trust and offer value in the process before we assume they would want to work with an agent. That being said, there will be the occasion when you catch a frustrated For Sale By Owner prospect on the right day, when they have already come to the conclusion that what they are doing is not working, so look for those signs and be prepared to list right away when possible. Most of these prospects, however, will require more value-building.

One way to start the conversation with a For Sale By Owner prospect is to ask for a tour of the home to preview for buyers in the area. It's important to let the prospect know that you will not ask them to list the property with you; you simply want to be knowledgeable about all the available inventory in your market to best serve your clients. This serves two purposes. The first is to put the prospect at ease. The second is to show them you will do whatever it takes — things other agents are not doing — to help your clients get what they want. Most agents working with buyer clients are not even looking outside of MLS. Here is a script:

Agent: "Hi, there. Are you the owner of 123 Main Street?"

Mr. or Mrs. FSBO: "Yes."

Agent: "I am calling because I have buyers searching in the area that we have not been able to find homes for, and I was hoping I could preview the property to see if might be a fit for one of my clients."

Mr. or Mrs. FSBO: "Why don't you just bring your client?"

Agent: "I will definitely bring them if it seems like the right fit for them. I have several clients looking in the area. The photos online do not always do justice to the home, so even though they may not have asked to see it yet, just by walking through it sometimes we find it would be perfect for one of them. If so, we will call them and schedule a showing. I could come by this afternoon at 2:00 P.M. or would tomorrow at 10:00 A.M. be better?"

(Always offer times in the middle of the day. If they are not available to show the property at those times that could be hurting their chances of selling. You may be able to later point out how having a listing agent who is available during the day could dramatically boost their response rate.)

Mr. or Mrs. FSBO: "You could come by this afternoon at 2:00 P.M., but we are not interested in listing with an agent."

Agent: "No problem. As I said earlier I promise to not even ask you to list the property. I look forward to meeting you at 2 P.M."

The Showing Appointment

The key to viewing the property is to look at it from a buyer's perspective, similar to what you would do during the beginning of a listing appointment. Remember that you promised them you would not ask them to list the property, so do not ask. This is the first step in showing your integrity and beginning to build trust. It's also important that you do have buyer leads looking in the area to build trust. You may even want to reference why the house may or may not work for some of your clients during your tour. Make notes about things that stand out. Compliment them about the great features of their home.

During and after the tour, use the time you have with the prospect to ask them questions that may uncover why they are selling and what they are doing to get the home sold. Questions you might ask include:

- This home is great. What made you decide to sell?
- Where will you be moving when the home sells?
- When would you like to be in your new home?
- What happens if the home doesn't sell?
- Just curious, how did you come up with the price?

- I found the home (by driving by, on Zillow, etc.); what other avenues are you using to market the property?
- How many showings have you had?
- How long have you been trying to sell?
- What type of feedback have you been getting?
- Have any agents been showing the property?

Once you have learned about the sellers' wants and needs and a little about how the process has been going for them, you have the opportunity to offer help before you leave. Depending on what their challenges have been, you could offer to drop off some different information either on staging or developing a marketing plan, or something else that may help them along the way. We are just looking for a way to add value. If they execute the plan you give them and they succeed in selling the home without you, then you have hopefully gained a relationship with them and earned their eternal gratitude. Maybe this will show up as referral business in the future. In most cases, they will not execute your plan because they either do not know how, do not have the time, or do not have some other resource. When they finally realize they cannot exercise the same marketing strategies you can that is when they will see your value.

Let them know that you will reach out to your buyer pool and see if there is any interest. You can even ask them if you could use their pictures or take some of your own to email blast out to all of your buyer leads in the database. There is a good chance some of your leads haven't seen this property. That means you have the opportunity to provide value to both your leads and the sellers at the same time.

Getting a Second Appointment

Find a reason to check back in with them. The next meeting should be to drop off whatever information you promised. Let them know you will connect with them based on any responses from your email blast. We want to build the relationship. When they are ready to list with an agent, you want to make sure they choose you. That will happen when you provide them with tons of value. They will have trust in you and see the value you bring to the table. Never leave a single meeting with them without a plan to follow up.

Marketing Listings to Create Leads

As we discussed in the chapter on secondary transactions, each listing presents an opportunity to meet new listing and buyer clients. Look to gain the permission of the seller to help them market their property. Depending on the laws in your state, you may be able to sign an agreement to market their property for buyer leads without representing the seller. This is clearly a calculated risk. You could end up bringing a buyer to them through another agent and earning nothing for your work. I would not agree to something like this in the long run, but it could be a powerful tool to get your foot in the door and show them your worth. Another option would be a short-term listing agreement. Maybe try a 30-day or even one-week listing agreement. In some areas where you are allowed to market with a coming soon campaign, you could potentially do a one-day listing agreement and promote the heck out of a single open house through online ads, MLS, circle prospecting, door-knocking, mailers, etc. This would create the same opportunity as a first open house at a new listing to meet buyer and seller leads. It also allows you to show these FSBO prospects your A game. If you create more traffic in one day than they have seen since listing the property, they may want to extend the listing so that you can help them get the property sold.

Overcoming the Pricing Objection

While a lack of marketing, the inability to make the home available for showings, and not being in MLS for buyer agents to find are all likely holding back the sale of this home, great deals tend to sell no matter what. If the home is sitting on the market as a For Sale By Owner, we can pretty much rest assured they missed the mark on price. This is not always the case, but most sellers believe—or want to believe—that their home is worth more than the actual market value.

This conversation can be tricky with a For Sale By Owner. Remember, the reason they did not want an agent was because they wanted to save money. Now, to work with you, not only are you going to require that they pay you a commission, but you are also likely asking them to lower the price of their home. There are two factors in addressing this issue that will soften the blow.

First, always get back to their motivation. No sellers get excited about selling their home. The work involved in preparing the house, packing everything, changing addresses, and organizing all the details is enough to stress anyone. People do not move because they want to sell their current home. People move because they want something better out there. They want a lower payment. They want more bedrooms. They want single-level living. They want maintenance-free living. They want a quiet neighborhood with a big yard. They want a shorter commute. They want better schools. These desires are the motivating factors that will create the inspiration to change the price if required to help them get there. We will need to remind them that our goal is to help them get to their goal through this real estate transaction. People do not say no to their own goals. The only way we can help them get there is to ask powerful questions to find their motivation and then dig deeper below the surface to find out why those things are important to them.

For example, when someone says they want a short commute, you want to know what about the shorter commute is important to them.

Agent: "What will having a shorter commute do for you?"

FSBO: "It will save me gas. It will put fewer miles on my car. It will save me time."

Agent: "Those are all great. What will you do with the extra time?"

FSBO: "Actually get to eat dinner with my family at night and put my kids to bed."

Agent: "What will that do for you and your family?"

FSBO: "It will make my relationship with all of them better."

Agents: "What happens if we don't find something, and the commute stays the way it is?"

FSBO: "It can't."

Ding. Ding. Ding. You found the motivation. While the shorter commute is great, the time with family is really the motivating factor. That is the non-negotiable that will make someone act. When we start discussing price, we want to know that price will help us to get the clients the shorter commute so they can spend more time with their family and eat dinner together.

The second factor in overcoming the pricing objection is evidence. People can argue opinions all day, but it is much harder to argue when physical evidence is placed in front of you. The best evidence will be comparable sales found in your local MLS. As we discussed earlier, knowing your market matters in your success as an agent. While having a handful of nearby comparable sales from

FOR SALE BY OWNER (FSBO)

the past few months is best for pricing a home, I have found that additional support of the selling price may be needed with prospects who have a strong difference of opinion. You may find it helpful to also pull current properties on the market in direct competition with the home. Also, expired and cancelled listings make for great lessons about what happens when an overpriced home sits on the market. Lastly, market history of sold homes will typically show the ones which sold quickly sold at or above the list price, while the ones that sat longer on the market tend to drop well below—and often close well below—their last listing price. Use this evidence to help support how a shift in price may be what it takes to help them achieve their goals.

Consistent contact and a soft approach to establish trust will open the door to working with some great For Sale By Owner clients. Even when you do not get the listing, you may find that in seeking to add value, you earn additional business from their unrepresented buyer leads or future referral business from the FSBO.

FSBO SUCCESS RITUALS

Daily:

- Search third-party sites like Zillow or Trulia for any listings posted For Sale By Owner.
- Call FSBO properties with "viewing for buyers" script.
- Use a dialer and lead provider like Vulcan 7 or Landvoice.

Weekly:

- Drive neighborhoods where you would like to take new listings searching for FSBOs.
- Visit any advertised FSBO open houses.
- Follow up with FSBO owners to continue building the relationship.
- Drop off items of value like marketing plans or staging tips.

Monthly/Quarterly:

- Send a market update or direct mail showing recently listed or sold properties in the neighborhood.

Chapter 14

EXPIRED LISTINGS

E xpired listings are the easiest sellers to find. You can search in the MLS for all expired listings in the past day, week, or month, and reach out to the sellers to see if they are still considering selling their home. The obstacle with these sellers is that many other agents will be contacting them at the same time, and often they will be upset with their agent as they could not sell the property as expected. While some listings expire because the agent did not do a great job with marketing or staging, oftentimes it is a hang-up of the seller that will stop the property from selling.

The first agent may have put the property under agreement in the first couple weeks as planned, and the seller may have been unwilling to negotiate after home inspection because they were newer to the market. After receiving the higher offer, they may have been unwilling to make the required pricing adjustments to accommodate the home inspection findings. The reason that the property did not sell does not matter. What matters is the seller's perception of why the property didn't sell. You could know from some research that their pricing was well over the market value, but the seller could well believe it was a lack of marketing. It's important that we start by asking the right questions to find out their motivation to sell and their perception of why the property didn't sell the first time.

Is the Seller Motivated?

It's important that we find the motivation for the seller. If they had somewhere they had planned on moving already, then they may be very motivated. They may already be past their intended deadline. It's possible they are carrying two payments or risk missing out on the home of their dreams that they have under contract. It's also possible that the reason they sat on the market so long without selling was a lack of clear motivation for selling in the first place. Keep in mind that there are good agents out there who still have listings that expire. They may have had a great marketing program in place for the property and just could not get the sellers to accept an offer for a fair price because they were not as motivated as they claimed.

Rather than waste a bunch of time, effort, energy, and money with unmotivated sellers, it will be worth your time to ask the following questions to determine if it makes sense to take expired listings.

- What made you put your home on the market in the first place?
- Where are you planning to move when your home sells?
- What about the new home excites you the most?
- If we put the home on the market and get an accepted offer right away, is moving in the next thirty days going to be a problem for you?
- What happens if the home doesn't sell?

As you work through these questions, you should get a good idea of whether the sellers were just testing the market to see if they could get a certain price that would make them move or if they have a serious plan to make a move. If they have bought into how the move will benefit them and they have a good reason for wanting to move, then we just need to figure out if we can make the numbers work for them based on the current market. There is an opportunity to gain trust with clients during this conversation when you are 100 percent honest with them about their situation. If selling will not allow them to get what they need or want, you should tell them.

Developing a New Plan

A seller whose home just sat on the market for 90 or 180 days will not want to hear the way to sell their property is another couple months of the same plan. We may have great ideas for getting the property sold. We may have bulletproof systems that work for us at getting homes sold, but with expired listings there is more information to uncover before pitching our marketing plan.

Ask the following questions to uncover what may or may not have been working and how much traffic or interest they may have had. There is no need to start over at the beginning again. Take advantage of the fact that we have market data for this specific home and ask:

- Did you have any offers on the property while it was on the market? What were the offers? Did you accept any or counter any? What happened?

- Approximately how many people came and physically viewed the property? How many in the first few weeks? How many in the last few weeks?

- What did you like about what your last agent did to market your property?
- Why do you think the property didn't sell?
- What would you like to have seen done differently?

These questions should allow you to get to know your client a little better – as well as their expectations for getting the property sold. I would almost never take out a newspaper ad to let people know about an open house because I know that I can reach far more people for far less money through online avenues. However, if a client let me know they believe the reason the property did not sell was because it was never advertised in the paper, you can bet that newspaper ads would become part of the strategy for selling that particular property as long as the seller was motivated to sell. If making the client feel heard and understood would only take a minor investment amounting to a small percentage of my commission, then it would be well worth the small shift in my marketing plan. We would still continue all the same online strategies we use in addition to the ad in the paper.

We also need to work with the client to help them re-frame the story of the property. Sometimes we need to change the marketing, other times the property needs staging, a few repairs, and some beautiful, professional photography. A renewed sense of energy around getting the property sold will go a long way in getting the listing signed and helping to create realistic expectations when you bring offers to the table. Whether you change the condition or the price of the property, something has to change to get the home under contract.

A New Market Analysis

Every expired listing should have a new market analysis completed. A lot of changes can happen in three to six months in the real estate world. If you were already overpriced by 5 percent and the market has shifted down by as little as 1 or 2 percent over the past few months that could be as much as 7 percent off from market value. If you have a $400,000 home, you could be $28,000 overpriced if you go on the market at the same price they started with last time. Not to mention that inventory may have changed. Being $28,000 over the market value may bring offers in a busy market with a limited inventory, but when seasonality kicks in to slow the market and inventory expands, that will price them outside of the market altogether.

Homes priced at or just below market value and look like the nicest homes in the price range sell the fastest and for the most money. The best value, in the form of the best house for the least money, will always sell the fastest. More people will want those homes, which will drive the purchase price up when combined with the right marketing plan to let everyone know the home is for sale.

You may need additional support for pricing adjustments with expired listings. Remember, another agent told them at one point that they could get that price for their home. Maybe they pushed against the initial suggestion of the first agent as well and talked them into trying for the higher price. Do not let the client push you into an overpriced listing. Show them why it did not work the first time and will not work now.

Finding Additional Expired Listing Opportunities

As we mentioned in the beginning of the chapter, the easiest expired listings to find are the ones that just came off the market. As recently as yesterday, these sellers were on the market trying to sell their home, and suddenly they are not. The challenge is that just about anyone in the entire MLS could be calling and sending them things at the same time. You should still reach out to these people as they are likely the most motivated, but there may be other opportunities to find.

Think about how market shifts affect pricing. Maybe some clients who couldn't sell a few years ago, during a shift in the market, may get a price that makes sense for them now that the market has recovered. A simple look back to when the market crashed in 2008 through the spiral down into 2011 will reveal a bunch of expired listings. Comparing that list to public record, we can check the last sale date to see if they ever came back on the market and sold. If they haven't come back on and sold, then we know at one point that seller wanted to sell and, based on appreciation from the past few years, we may be able to achieve a sale price that could help them get what they want. There will not be as much competition in reaching out to these past expired listings, making it easier to get their attention. Now we need to find out if they are motivated to sell now.

Standing Out from the Crowd

Regardless of whether you are reaching out to fresh expired listings or expired listings from years past, you will need to stand out to get the appointment. Consider what these potential seller clients might look for in a new agent. If they felt like their last agent lacked follow-up or were not aggressive enough in their marketing efforts, then they may well be looking to fill that void. Consider that in your efforts to schedule listing appointments with these prospects.

You may need to leave several messages. You may need to knock on their door. If you show up at the door, be prepared for a listing consultation on the spot. You may not get a second chance. Several of these newly expired listings will come back on the market quickly, so make sure not to hesitate in reaching out. Then, once you reach out, do not give up until they are either back on market or have let you know that they changed their plans about selling. Bottom line: you can tell people that your follow-up skills will help get their home sold or you can show them. Showing them may very well get you a listing opportunity you may have otherwise missed out on.

Lastly, handwritten notes are always a great way to stand out in any crowd. People can tell the difference between the form letters and emails that replace the first name at the top and a personalized, handwritten note. How will you stand out with your expired listing prospects?

EXPIRED LISTINGS SUCCESS RITUALS

Daily:

- Search MLS for all expired listings.
- Call expired listings.
- Use a dialer and lead provider like Vulcan 7 or LandVoice.

Weekly:

- Mail postcard or letter to expired listings until back on market.
- Drop off items of value like marketing plans or staging tips.
- Knock on doors of expired listings.

Monthly/Quarterly:

- Reach out to any expired listings from past three months that have not yet come back on the market. Most agents will have given up by now.

Chapter 15

WORKING WITH INVESTORS

nvestor clients are a different animal than your typical retail clients who are buying and selling homes. For most clients, there will be an emotional component to buying and selling real estate. Sellers may have a personal connection to a property since they may have shared special memories in the house. Buyers will gain excitement for the right property. Most investors will look at the property based on whether adding this purchase to their portfolio will help them reach their financial goals. This is not to say that working with investors is easier or harder, only that it is different.

While working with investors comes down to whether or not the numbers work, one thing that does not change for the agent regardless of your client is that the better you get at asking the right questions to find out what your client wants, the more success you will find in real estate. This is especially true if your client believes you understand their goals and have the ability to help them achieve those objectives through real estate.

Why Investors?

New client acquisition is important in any business, and client retention grows profits through repeat clients and orders. While repeat clients are important in the real estate field, the average homeowner is only buying a new property every seven to ten years.

Working with investors creates a unique opportunity because they are far more likely to buy multiple units in one year. They may even sell units to buy other units that create better profits. Some investors will flip properties repeatedly, allowing for repeat business in both the purchasing side and new listings. Using the skills in the chapter on secondary transactions, we can turn many of those listings into additional new clients.

Investors create many opportunities to grow your business. The lifetime value of these clients can be hundreds of thousands or even millions in commissions. That frees you up to spend a little more in order to find these clients. Consider if you had an investment client looking to buy a single-family or multi-family property. You could mail out to homeowners letting them know that you have a client looking to buy properties just like theirs. Now, instead of just asking them to list their property, you can ask them if you can bring a buyer to them before they could even hit the market. Sometimes, this will help you in finding your investors great deals. In other instances, your buyer may choose not to purchase the property, but the seller may want to list their property with you, anyway. Working with investors creates these unique opportunities if you leverage them.

Where Do We Find Investor Clients?

When most people think of investor clients, they think of flippers, buy-and-hold investors who will work with anyone that can bring them a deal, or the builder/developer who will work with anyone that can bring them the land. While I wouldn't discourage working with these clients because they can offer tremendous opportunities, these are not the only investor clients.

In an interview with investor agent Gary Wilson, Gary talks about how he built his business to over 100 units a year without a team, by finding investor clients. Gary shares some of his ideas on our online resource page (www.explosivesalesgrowth.com/realestate). One of the most interesting things I learned from Gary was how he found his investor clients. Gary would send out packages of information with a cover letter sharing how he would help his clients find investment properties, along with some deals currently or recently found in MLS. He would even break down the numbers on some deals so prospects could see how they could increase their net worth through real estate investing.

While anyone could save the money required to place a down payment on an investment property, 25 percent might be a substantial amount for many. That is why you should focus on high-income earners, especially small business owners. People like dentists, orthodontists, engineers, and other similar career paths make for great potential investor clients. Not only do many of them already own the building where they operate their business, they also make a significant income and could potentially put down large sums for a down payment on investment property. Because they likely work in their business, most are busy and will appreciate the assistance of a great agent in helping to grow their investment portfolio. You then have the opportunity to help them leverage real estate investing to create freedom through passive income.

The Overlooked Investor/Retail Client

"House hacking" is the term for purchasing a single-family or multi-family home to live in while renting out the other units, bedrooms, or both to pay for the house so the owner can live for little or no expense. House hacking presents an amazing opportunity for anyone with the freedom and flexibility to share their space. If they are willing to move every so often, then they may add more than one property to their portfolio.

As the cost of homes in some large cities and suburban areas moves out of reach for lower-income earners, house hacking offers a unique strategy to help your clients get into homes they may not otherwise be able to afford. By taking the leap to get into a larger single- or multi-family home, the client may have the opportunity to live with less expenses than they may have been paying in rent while increasing their net worth over time through debt pay-down and potential appreciation. These clients will hopefully get the taste for investing and what it can do for them. From there, you will likely have the opportunity to help them continue growing their portfolio in the future. These prospects can be targeted online or through mailings to apartment buildings. Conversations at open houses with first-time homebuyers may lend themselves to this opportunity.

Providing Information and Tools

Holding a regular investor club meeting or even just a training event for people who are considering their first real estate investment will create opportunities to meet these potential clients. Providing them information about the current market, lending options, and existing investment opportunities will create value for these prospects before they ever become your clients.

You may teach them how to use an investment spreadsheet to evaluate a deal or even build a pro forma to show them how an investment might impact their net worth. You could teach them how to measure ROI, cap rates, and even the cash-on-cash return based on the amount of down payment they choose. A higher down payment could mean more cash flow now or it could allow for a shorter repayment term, allowing for less interest paid and creating a higher cash flow at the end of the term. This strategy will lower cash-on-cash return in the early years since they will be laying out more of their own cash up front. Different investors will have different goals, and you will need to learn the tools of the trade to be able to help them achieve those goals.

If you are looking for a crash course on real estate investing, there are several books that we recommend on our reading list, which you will find on the website so we can keep the list up-to-date as new resources become available.

With the right investor clients, you can build a consistent business with repeat clients who create opportunities for you to meet new clients through their listings. Rather than constantly seeking new clients, you could sell the same clients two, three, five, or even twenty or thirty homes in a single year. It may open the door for you to help other investors unload an entire portfolio all at once. I spoke with an investor agent just yesterday that is closing a 22-unit portfolio for over $4 million in volume. For some agents that would be an entire year's worth of selling homes.

As your investor clients build a portfolio over time, they will likely sell off some of their initial, smaller buildings and roll that money over into larger buildings that have more units and create more profit. As you help them build their portfolio, they will continue to help you grow your business each year as well.

INVESTOR AGENT SUCCESS RITUALS

Daily:

- Search MLS for any new potential investment opportunities.

Weekly:

- Reach out to investor clients with potential opportunities.
- Post pictures, videos, and articles about investment properties you are touring or listing.
- Send email invites to investing informational sessions.
- Post your meet-up group and informational sessions online and on social media sites.
- Send letters or handwritten notes to potential listings that match your investor clients needs.

Monthly/Quarterly:

- Mail potential investment packages to targeted prospective investors.
- Host local investor meet-up or investing information session.
- Write articles and blog posts that would attract investor clients.

Chapter 16

MEASURING YOUR RETURN

Congratulations on making it to the end of all the lead generation strategies. You are ready to implement and dive deeper into a few key areas to help you grow your real estate business. While lead generation is an important part of growing a successful business, it is not the only qualification. The way we can measure the success of a business is to determine whether it is profitable. Remember, you are working to build a lifestyle, and your lifestyle will likely require money to build.

You need to choose the two or three lead generation sources you will focus on for mastery. You have the scripts and tools ready and waiting for you. These methods will work, so you just need to choose the strategies that are right for you based on your business and how well they suit your personality and strengths.

You will also need to decide based on your current business if you need immediate deals or if you have the time to build a longer-term strategy. Maybe you will decide on a mix of both. Developing online leads through natural organic search may take time while calling FSBO's and expired listings is more likely to provide immediate business. Your sphere of influence is also likely to provide immediate business, especially when you include referral business.

Finally, you will need to decide if you have more time or money to invest. Some lead generation strategies we discussed will take only your time and little money. Others, like direct mail, will be more leveraged activities that require far less time, but they will require a larger investment of cash.

These components should help you decide which lead generation strategies to use in building your business plan. Keep in mind that the activities you will actually complete are the ones that belong in your plan. If you have added FSBO calls to your lead generation plan for the last three years and you have yet to call one, then choose a different strategy.

Regardless of which strategies you choose, it is important that we measure whether every dollar we send out into our business brings back additional dollars to help it grow. We are looking for our money to return at least three times to five times our investment. You may allow for a lower return for the less time-intensive leads, especially listing leads. For example, a three times return on investment may be great in farming where there is little follow-up required (small time investment) and most of the leads are listing leads. On the other hand, you may be looking for more like four to five times the return from online leads that require lots of calls and emails to convert and may bring more buyer clients.

Profit and Loss Report (P&L) as a Decision-Making Tool

There have been plenty of agents out there who earn a ton in commissions simply because they spend a lot of money. To be profitable, you need to measure your income and expenses regularly. You need to look at each expense as an investment and hold it accountable to bringing additional money back into the business. This will help ensure that you run a profitable business to create the life of your dreams.

I will use the example of the GPS here. Most people have a GPS – whether it is in their car or on their phone. The great part of the GPS is that it gets us where we want to go. The GPS only requires three pieces of information to make this work. First, it needs a starting point. Your starting point comes from having clarity about where you are in the business. What worked for you last year? Where are you struggling?

The second bit of information is the end point. Where is it you are trying to go? Your end point is your goal for the year. The GPS has a map or plan based on your preferences. Do you want to avoid tolls or freeways? Is the distance traveled or time on the road more important? This book will help you create your plan for real estate success as long as you choose your top three lead generation strategies and fill your mornings with activities from each of those chapters.

The last strength of the GPS, the real magic, is that whenever you get off course, the GPS knows you are off track, recalculates, and gives you an immediate plan to get back on track. By constantly measuring our numbers, we have the ability to never veer too far off course.

> If you measure yearly, you can have a bad year.
> If you measure monthly, you can have a bad month.
> If you measure weekly, you can have a bad week.
> If you measure daily, you can have a bad day.
> —Unknown

I would rather have a bad day than a bad year. When I ask in trainings for agents to raise their hands if they complete a Profit and Loss (P&L) report in their business, only about 25 percent of the room raises their hands. When I ask how many of those complete them monthly rather than annually while completing their taxes, about half of the hands go down. If agents are not completing this report on a monthly basis, they have no tools available to them to make intelligent spending decisions to grow their business.

You can use any model you like, but I will use the numbers from *The Millionaire Real Estate Agent*. If you consider that your two largest operating expenses will be administrative salaries and lead generation, then just knowing your numbers should help you make decisions around when to invest in your business by adding more leverage and/or more marketing dollars. By assuming a budget of 10 to 12 percent of GCI (Gross Commissions Income) as a starting point, a quick glance at our P&L should tell us if we are in a position to increase marketing dollars or add a new administrative assistant or marketing person to our team. Without this report, we may not even be certain of our income for the year, let alone what we have already spent on marketing. When we start taking our work seriously, as a business, we will hold each of these decisions accountable to the money they return to the business. If we aren't willing to ensure that we are profitable, then what is the point of working every day? Would you go to a job every day if you weren't sure you were getting paid?

Once you measure your income and expenses, you can make adjustments to grow your business faster. Only spend money as it comes in. Do not just assume a budget based on your goal. Also, make sure you have the cash to carry the longer-term lead generation plans for the time it will take to see a return on the investment. There is no sense spending money on farming for three months if you are not sure you can afford the fourth month.

Key Performance Indicators

Aside from measuring just income and expenses, you will need to measure the following categories to determine which of your lead generation techniques is creating the greatest return on your investment. If you find that one strategy is working well, you may increase your investment in that one area. This can help you grow your business even faster to new levels of profit.

- **Leads**—How many leads are created from each source? You will need to decide based on each source what constitutes a lead. What information will you need to collect for it to count as an actual lead?

- **Calls/Contacts**—How many calls or points of contact did you have with each type of lead for the day, week, or month? You are measuring your activity because you have to complete the follow-up before you decide if a lead generation source is working. If you want to increase conversion rates and profitability, working on your scripts and follow-up plans will improve both. Remember that your goal here is an appointment, so you want to measure your number of contacts against the number of appointments set to help determine if the method is working for you.

- **Appointments**—How many appointments did you set from each lead source? How many appointments do you need per week or month to hit your goals? Qualifying your leads may lower your number of appointments but improve your conversion on the appointments. Improving your buyer and seller consultations will increase your appointment conversions. This will come from practicing those consultations. Work on the needs analysis and building value.

- **Listings/Buyers Signed**—This is how many buyer agreements and listing agreements you signed from each lead generation source. This will let you know which sources are producing the most viable leads.

- **Listings/Buyers Sold**—This statistic will let you know how much income you are bringing back to your business from each of the lead generation categories. This is how we will measure our return on investment. For each buyer and listing sold, we will need to know our commission to determine the ROI.

Combining Lead Generation with Measurement Tools

The key to implementing this book is to go through the book and implement in order. You should start by creating positive personal habits that will start your day on the right foot. Establish the right mindset, determine your vision and lifestyle goals and set appropriate business goals based on what you want. Then you will put your basic systems in place to manage your time and database.

Once the basics are in place, you will need to build your business plan based on putting three lead generation strategies into place to support you in hitting your goals. Take the time to learn the scripts for each of those prospects. Continue mastering the scripts and tools in your key areas without stopping to check out every shiny object. Put the daily, weekly, and monthly tasks in your calendar. Then take action. Make the calls, send the notes, write the blog, post the ad, and then follow up until the closing and beyond.

Congratulations on reading the book to the end. You have all the tools you need to increase your leads, take more listings, and build the six-figure business of your dreams. I look forward to connecting with you in our online community at www.explosivesalesgrowth.com/community. Also, please don't forget to check out the additional resources for scripts, tools, and video interviews at www.explosivesalesgrowth.com/realestate.

END OF BOOK NOTES

As someone who spent three years managing a real estate offices to complete over 2,000 transactions for more than $1 Billion in real estate sales, I am excited to share this book with you, so it may help you create consistency in your business and break through your current ceiling of income.

I am currently in my own transition having recently quit that management role to pursue my full-time career in writing books, speaking, and coaching. I know the difficulty in committing to an entrepreneurial position like the role of real estate agent, and I hope this book will help you to hang in there long enough to reap the rewards.

I look forward to spending more time travelling and learning with my wife, Mary Lynn, and our three children Connor, Lily, and Harrison. I hope you build a business that allows you the freedom to spend time doing the things you enjoy as well. We just finished a short trip to the White Mountains where the deer walked right up to our window. There is a great picture of my kids watching the deer with the mountains in the background. You can see it on Instagram. Follow me there at snowpants1204.

You can also connect with me via email at ryan@explosivesales-growth.com. I look forward to hearing from you.

A SPECIAL INVITATION FROM RYAN

Having mentored thousands of agents as a real estate sales trainer and coach, I understand the importance of accountability and community when implementing any new strategies. As a co-author of *The Miracle Morning for Salespeople*, I have seen the power a supportive online community provides when building new habits.

I am personally inviting you to join our online community of like-minded salespeople to share ideas and learn from one another during the process of implementing the strategies in this book.

Just go to **www.explosivesalesgrowth.com/community** and request to join the Explosive Sales Growth Community online. The people in this community are dedicated to building a real estate business that supports the life of their dreams.

I will be moderating the community and checking in regularly. I look forward to seeing you there!

ABOUT THE AUTHOR

Ryan Snow is a #1 Best-Selling Author, Sales Leader, Business Coach, and Teacher at heart. With over ten years in a classroom or training room and several more as a business coach and mentor, Ryan's mission is to help people achieve extraordinary results in life and in sales, through personal and professional development.

Ryan's first book, *The Miracle Morning for Salespeople* with Hal Elrod and Honorée Corder, expands on Hal's original Miracle Morning message of exponential growth by seizing the first vital hours of the morning, connecting that personal development with professional development and habits to increase sales.

If you are interested in speaking with Ryan about sales and accountability coaching, you can find him on Instagram at @Snowpants1204 or email ryan@explosivesalesgrowth.com.

Suggested Titles by the Author

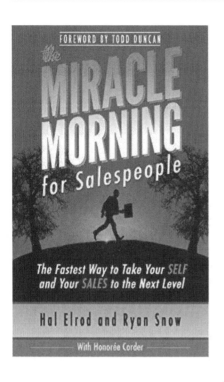

Ready to Go from 'Average' Salesperson to 'Top Performer?'

The Miracle Morning for Salespeople brings you these Life S.A.V.E.R.S. as a guide for taking your SALES to the next level. Get beyond the typical sales advice and get into a daily rhythm that will transform your career.

Welcome to The Miracle Morning for Salespeople Companion Guide.

This Companion Guide was designed to help you implement the teachings of The Miracle Morning for Salespeople at a high level by working through over 120 pages of exercises. We don't want these lessons to be left on the bookshelf. Increase your sales now.

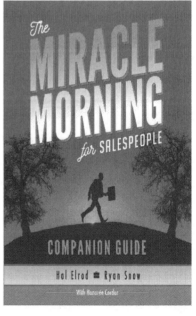

EXPLOSIVE
SALES GROWTH
IN REAL ESTATE

GENERATE MORE LEADS, TAKE MORE LISTINGS,
AND BUILD A SIX-FIGURE INCOME

Bulk Order Form

Get a Copy for your entire Real Estate Office and Save!

Your agents will learn how to:
- Use mindset and attitude to accelerate your career
- Create a daily success ritual, building habits and routines
- Grow influence—build a better network and increase your reach
- Develop and implement a lead generation plan to take more listings
- Measure ROI and understand their results and refine their approach

Name

Email

Mobile

Shipping Address

City, State, Zip

Credit Card Number

Expiration Date   Security Code

Billing Zip Code

Signature

Retail Price: $19.97

25-99	$15
100-249	$12
250-499	$10
500-999	$9
1000 - 4999	$8
5000 - 9999	$7
10,000+	$6

*Shipping charges are additional. Please inquire for rates.
**For autographed copies, please add $5 per book.

Quantity: _____

Please email to ryan@explosivesalesgrowth.com   Subject: ESGRE Bulk Order

Book Ryan to Speak

Ryan Snow is a #1 Best-Selling Author, Sales Leader, Business Coach, and Teacher at heart. With over seven years in a classroom and several more as a business coach and mentor, his mission is to help people achieve extraordinary results in life and in sales through personal and professional development. Ryan led a brokerage to over $1 Billion in sales in the last 3 years with over $20 Million in commissions.

Popular Workshops, Seminars, and Keynotes

The Miracle Morning for Salespeople Workshop
Designing a Focused Lead Generation Plan
5 Principles of Self-Leadership
Understanding Motivation - Step Out of Your Comfort Zone

"Ryan is a World--Class Sales Trainer. His ability to connect the benefits of a powerful morning routine to specific sales habits that will grow your business is guaranteed to impact your sales results!"
– Hal Elrod

"Ryan connects. His ideas inspire action and his program keeps delivering long after the event." **– Jon Vroman**

www.explosivesalesgrowth.com/speaking